Fundamentals of Transport Economics

Fundamentals of Transport Economics

STEPHEN GLAISTER

St. Martins Press · New York

Printed in Great Britain

First published in the United States of America in 1981

Library of Congress Card Catalog Number 81-52183

ISBN 0-312-31152-4

Contents

Preface   ix

Acknowledgements   xiii

1 **Introduction and Survey**   1

    1.1   The demand curve   1
    1.2   The price elasticity of demand   3
    1.3   Marginal revenue   5
    1.4   Marginal cost   6
    1.5   Price discrimination   6
    1.6   Peak loads   7
    1.7   Perfect competition   7
    1.8   Consumer surplus   8

2 **Consumer Behaviour and the Demand Curve**   13

    2.1   Consumer preferences   15
    2.2   The 'standard' consumer analysis   16
    2.3   Properties of demand functions   18
    2.4   The indirect utility function   23
    2.5   The dual approach: the expenditure function   23
    2.6   Consumer surplus   25
    2.7   The multiple price change case   27
    2.8   Aggregation   29
    2.9   The evaluation of service quality changes   30

3 The Producer   34

3.1   Revenue   34
3.2   Costs   37
3.3   The long run and short run   40
3.4   Perfect competition   43
3.5   The supply function   45
3.6   Monopolistic behaviour   45
3.7   Market equilibrium and comparative statics   48

4 Welfare Economics   53

4.1   The conditions necessary for economic efficiency   54
4.2   The fundamental theorem   57

5 Marginal Social Cost Pricing   61

5.1   Congestion of homogeneous traffic flows   61
5.2   Peak load pricing   65
5.3   Pricing subject to financial constraint   76
5.4   Non-homogeneous traffic congestion: an example of second best pricing   80
5.5   The integration of second best with peak pricing: an example   86
5.6   Problems   91

6 Queues   94

6.1   Random processes   94
6.2   General queues   98
6.3   Special cases   100
6.4   Waiting times   101
6.5   The distribution of the queue length and waiting times   103
6.6   Airport runway capacity: an example   104
6.7   Problems   106

7 Car Ownership, Discrete Choices and Travel Demand   108

7.1   The logistic function   110
7.2   The application to car ownership forecasting   112
7.3   Individual household based models   116

7.4 Durables 121
7.5 Behavioural travel demand models 127

8 **Economic Evaluation, Investment Criteria and Public Enterprise Objectives** 140

8.1 Present value maximization 140
8.2 Corporate objectives 146
8.3 The differences implied by differing objectives: an illustration 151
8.4 Income redistribution 154
8.5 The choice of service quality 158
8.6 Problems 162

9 **Intervention: Regulation, Taxation and Subsidy** 164

9.1 Tendency to monopoly 165
9.2 Safety 168
9.3 Imperfect information, risk and uncertainty 169
9.4 Coordination and unfair competition 170
9.5 Cross-subsidy 172
9.6 Externalities 173
9.7 Dynamic instabilities 174
9.8 National considerations 174
9.9 Theories of regulation 174
9.10 The costs of regulation 177

Bibliography 184

Index 191

Preface

Applied economics is becoming an increasingly quantitative subject. This is particularly so in the field of transport where the physical systems involved are capable of generating a great deal of quantitative information in addition to that provided on economic and social performance by routine ticketing information and by the many surveys that are carried out. Those who have to plan new facilities or to manage existing ones tend to want quantitative answers to quantitative questions: 'by how much will revenue increase and patronage fall if we increase fares by 10%?', 'if subsidies are increased by £10m per annum by how much will fares be reduced, how many more vehicles will we need and will there be sufficient benefit to congested traffic to justify the extra public expenditure?', 'if we build a new bridge or a bypass will the time savings that this allows be of sufficient value to justify the cost and what toll should we charge?', 'by how much will queueing time be reduced at this port in the summer peak if we invest in an extra vessel?'

A high proportion of those who have to answer this kind of question have considerable quantitative skills by virtue of a primary training in engineering, natural science, mathematics or statistics. But it is much rarer that they have a specialist qualification in economics and they rely on a knowledge picked up in the course of their work. The Advisory Committee on Trunk Road Assessment (1977) found that of the 3282 people engaged in the planning and design of UK trunk roads only eight were economists or statisticians and none of those were situated away from the headquarters of the

Department of Transport. This in spite of the fact that it had
for some time been a requirement for all trunk road schemes
to be given a formal economic assessment.

This has meant that people faced with particular economic
problems have had to find their way through a large economics literature, not all of it relevant to their particular needs
and little of it exploiting their particular skills in mathematical technique. I hope that this book will be of some help in
such circumstances. The book may also be of interest to final
year undergraduates and postgraduate students of Transport
Engineering, Transport Planning and Transport Economics and
to students of Public Finance, Public Enterprise Economics
and Economic Theory in general who are looking for examples
of how their subject may be applied.

My aim has been to write a concise book in a way that will
be readily accessible to those with a familiarity with mathematical and quantitative methods. I am particularly anxious
to clarify the relationships between the techniques which
have become commonplace in applied work and their underlying theoretical origins. These are not always fully appreciated
and I think that this has frequently been a source of mis-
understanding about what economics claims – and does not
claim –. to say. A good example is the relationship between
consumer surplus, which is frequently used in estimating the
benefits of a pricing or investment proposal, and the theory
of consumer preferences which 'justifies' it. In order to do
this I have provided an account of the standard theory of the
consumer, of the producer and of Welfare Economics in
chapters 2, 3 and 4. The economist will find this material
familiar and may want to skip it. Chapter 1 provides a brief
survey of the material in the rest of the book.

The book has developed from a course of lectures for final
year undergraduates and graduate students taking an option
in Transport Economics at the London School of Economics.
It should not be regarded as a self-contained text in the subject. There are many important topics which are not covered
and which are adequately discussed in a variety of other
texts. I have provided full references to the bibliography
throughout the text so as to direct the interested reader to
basic material which is omitted here and to research topics in

the journals. Examples of good basic texts in Transport Economics are Thomson (1974), Gwilliam and Mackie (1975), Mohring (1976); Stubbs, Tyson and Dalvi (1980). Rees (1976) is a useful text on Public Enterprise Economics and Atkinson and Stiglitz (1980) give a very complete account of the theory of Public Finance which is fundamental to much of this book. The basic mathematical requirement is a familiarity with the multivariate calculus. A little matrix algebra is used in chapter 2 but this is in a section which could be skipped by the reader without great loss.

I am grateful to a publisher's reader and to many students for comments on drafts of material for this book. I am particularly indebted to colleagues with whom I have collaborated in research mentioned at several points and to Barbara Hammond and Sheila Collins for their excellent secretarial assistance.

Acknowledgements

I am grateful to the following for permission to reproduce in this book material which has previously appeared elsewhere: *Journal of Transport Economics and Policy, Economic Journal, Journal of Public Economics, American Economic Review*, and the University of London for some questions that have appeared on examination papers.

1 Introduction and Survey

The purpose of this chapter is to give an introductory survey
of the material contained in the remainder of this book.

1.1 The demand curve

Throughout we are concerned with analysing markets in
which services are bought and sold.

We are interested in *predicting* what will happen to traffic
as the result of such things as fare changes, income changes,
tax changes, service quality changes, and government regulation. Very often we are further concerned with *evaluation*
and *prescription*. We wish to be able to say whether a new
investment such as a road or a bridge would be a 'good
thing' in some sense. We would also wish to be able to discuss
the merit of subsidy and regulation by licensing or other
means which restricts competition. For both prediction and
evaluation one is inevitably driven to a consideration of
individual consumer behaviour: to make useful predictions we
must assume that individuals behave in a reasonably consistent manner, and the only scientific way to evaluate is to
attempt to relate what happens to the personal preferences of
the people affected.

The aim of chapter 2 is to show that the market demand
curve summarizes a considerable amount of information
concerning consumer behaviour and to show how the curve's
properties are related to those of the underlying consumer
preferences. The demand curve is illustrated in figure 1.1. It is
defined to be *a relation between price charged and the*

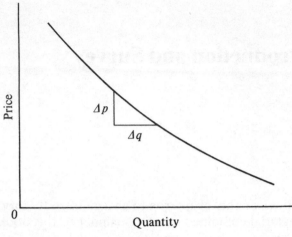

Figure 1.1

number of trips per unit time consumers would like to make at that price. It is drawn with a negative slope everywhere, indicating the assumption (discussed in chapter 2) that, other things being held constant, a higher price will mean a lower demand.

Because the relationship is monotonic (i.e. single sloped) it may be 'inverted' and interpreted as giving the price at which a given number of trips could be sold. Adopting the usual convention that the independent variable should be represented on the horizontal axis this would be the interpretation appropriate to the diagram as shown. However, in many discussions it is more natural to regard the fare as the independent variable, in which case the diagram is drawn 'on its side'.

Note that the curve is a notional concept in that it may not be technically possible to supply some of the quantities implied. It represents quantities consumers would *like* to consume at various prices. Note also that it is drawn on the assumption that all other relevant variables are held constant. Such other variables would include prices of other goods and services, personal incomes, advertising, and service quality. If any of these were to change then the curve would move. For instance, if advertising were to be increased then one would expect more units to be demanded at each price and so the curve would move to the right. Conversely any analysis using this curve is a *partial* analysis since the effects on the quantities of *other* goods consumed and on employee's incomes are ignored, as are the implications for the resources which will have to be transferred from or to the activity under consideration as the quantity consumed changes.

In practice one often cannot hope to know what a large portion of the demand curve looks like. Rather one is concerned with the *change* in demand that can be expected in response to a relatively small *change* in price. This is summarized by the rate of change of demand which is given by the ratio $\Delta q/\Delta p$ in the diagram. This is also known as the *slope* of the curve. In the limiting case where the price change becomes indefinitely small this also becomes the *derivative* of the quantity with respect to the price. Unless the demand curve is a straight line the slope will change as the price changes.

1.2 The price elasticity of demand

Although it is a fundamental quantity, the slope of the demand curve is of limited use in some situations because of the units it implicitly carries. The statement that in a certain city an increase of one penny per mile in the average bus fare would be expected to cause a loss of 1.4 million passengers per week is not very informative on its own. To assess its importance one needs to know the current fare level and the current level of patronage. Suppose that the proposal is to increase the fare from 5 pence to 6 pence per passenger mile and that the fall in patronage is expected to be from 20 million to 18.6 million passenger miles a week. Then a 20% fare increase is causing a 7% patronage fall. Hence a 1% fare increase would cause approximately 0.35% patronage fall. In this case we say that the *elasticity of demand* is -0.35. This is a unitless quantity which has a meaning even if the levels of the variables are not specified.

The price elasticity of demand, η, is defined to be *the percentage change in demand caused by a 1% change in price*:

$$\eta = \frac{\% \text{ change in demand}}{\% \text{ change in demand}} = \frac{(\Delta q/q) \times 100}{(\Delta p/p) \times 100} = \frac{\Delta q}{\Delta p} \frac{p}{q}$$

(1.1)

In the notation of the calculus (1.1) may be written as

$$\eta = \frac{dq}{dp} \frac{p}{q} = \frac{d \log q}{d \log p}$$

(1.2)

In general, just as the slope of the curve will vary with price, so will the elasticity. There is, however, one class of demand functions, of the form

$$q = ap^{-\epsilon}$$

(1.3)

where a and ϵ are positive constants, for which the elasticity is $-\epsilon$ and is therefore independent of price. (Note that on the convention adopted in this book a price elasticity is a *negative* number, indicating that quantity goes *down* as price goes *up*.)

If at some point on a demand curve $\eta = -1$ we say that it has unit elasticity at that point. If $\eta > -1$ (or equivalently $|\eta| < 1$) we say that the elasticity is low or that the *demand is inelastic* because the quantity is relatively unresponsive to price. If on the other hand $\eta < -1$ (or $|\eta| > 1$) then the elasticity is high and the demand is said to be *elastic*. The value quoted above for urban bus systems of about $-1/3$ has been found to be a typical value occurring with remarkable frequency around the world; Bly (1976) gives a survey. A more representative value for intercity rail in the United Kingdom might be of the order of -0.8 and recent experience on the North Atlantic air routes might suggest substantially higher elasticities.

It is also useful to define elasticities with respect to variables other than price. Thus the income elasticity is the percentage increase in demand associated with a 1% increase in income, holding prices constant.

Incidentally, it is convenient to always talk of price and income changes *in real terms*, that is, after allowing for any changes in the general price level due to inflation. If a fare rises at the same percentage rate as all other prices and incomes, there is no change in real prices or real incomes. If money fares are held constant over a period of general inflation then there will be a fall in real fares and an increase in demand may be expected. This phenomenon was observed during the mid-1970s period of general price restraint which was imposed on many UK operators. The Price Commission Report on London Transport Fares (1978b), gives a good illustration of this. The theoretical basis is discussed further under the heading of *homogeneity of demand* in chapter 2. Its implications for public transport policy are discussed in chapter 9.

1.3 Marginal revenue

The *revenue* of an operator is the product of price and quantity:

$$R = pq \qquad (1.4)$$

The *marginal revenue* (MR) is the *change in revenue which will occur if the operator reduces his price sufficiently to sell just one more unit*. It is shown in section 3.1 that

$$MR = p(1 + 1/\eta) \qquad (1.5)$$

This states that the change in revenue from selling one more unit is the price obtained from that unit less an amount depending on the elasticity of demand. The price has had to be lowered to sell the extra unit so that revenue is lost on all the other units. For instance, if the fare is 5p and the elasticity is $-1/3$ then the marginal revenue is $5[1 + (-3)]$p or -10p per extra unit sold. In this case a price fall causes a fall in revenue and conversely a price rise would cause an increase in revenue. On the other hand if the elasticity were -2 then the marginal revenue would be $+2.5$p, so that a price rise would reduce revenue because so much traffic would be lost.

In general, if the demand is inelastic then a price rise will cause a rise in revenue, whilst if demand is elastic a price rise will cause a fall in revenue. There has been a long-standing debate between the rail unions and management about whether fares should be raised or lowered in order to increase revenue. This can be precisely characterized as a dispute about whether the elasticity of demand is greater than or less than one at the current fare level.

1.4 Marginal cost

In almost all situations it is not only the change in revenue that an action will cause that must be considered. The change in costs is equally relevant because typically one is interested in the change in revenue net of costs, that is, the change in profit. *Marginal cost* is defined to be the *change in total costs caused by the supply of one more unit*; that is, the rate of change of costs with respect to output. It is also known as the *avoidable* cost of the extra unit of output.

Suppose now that an operator wishes to choose his price and output so as to maximize his profit. If, at some level of traffic his marginal revenue exceeds his marginal costs, then by lowering his price a little so as to sell extra units his revenue will increase by more than his costs. Hence his profit will increase. Conversely, if marginal revenue is less than marginal cost he can increase profit by raising price and reducing output. At a profit maximum therefore it must be the case that marginal revenue and marginal cost (MC) are equal. In other words,

$$p(1 + 1/\eta) = MC \qquad\qquad (1.6)$$

This fact has two implications which we shall discuss in detail in later chapters. One is that an operator who adopts this rule will choose a price which is above his marginal cost. The second is that since it normally costs more to produce more, marginal cost will be positive and thus marginal revenue must also be positive. So we would not expect to find a profit maximizing operator working at a point where the price elasticity of demand is less than unity.

1.5 Price discrimination

It follows that if an operator can separate his market into two or more distinct sub-markets each having different price elasticities, it will pay him to charge different prices even though the costs of supply may be very similar. This is known as *price discrimination* or 'charging what the market will bear'. Examples are the provision of first and second class facilities, the granting of fare concessions to groups such as students and the elderly (who normally have to prove that they are *bona fide* members of their respective groups by producing an identification card) and the sale of cheap air tickets on terms which suit holidaymakers but rule out short-stay business travellers. Another example is the charging of different fares on different routes depending on how severe the competition is. If a rail route is paralleled by a motorway and an air service then the price elasticity as seen by the railway will be relatively high because a given price increase will cause a relatively big loss of passengers to the competition. If there is no competition then the elasticity will be relatively low and a higher price can be charged. In fact the inverse of the demand elasticity provides a useful index of 'market power' or 'monopoly power'.

Price discrimination on these grounds has often been regarded as 'unfair' or against 'the public interest' and has therefore attracted the attention of regulatory authorities. These matters are discussed in chapters 5 and 9.

1.6 Peak loads

It also follows from (1.6) that prices will vary if marginal costs of supply vary, even if demand characteristics do not. The most obvious example of this is the peak or 'rush hour'. Because the supply of an extra trip in the peak requires the provision of more capacity, marginal costs are high relative to the off-peak when they may even be negligible. The fact that many operators do not charge full peak marginal costs simply indicates that they are not behaving as profit maximizers for one reason or another. The economics of the peak are discussed in chapter 5 and the various objectives operators might adopt are discussed in chapters 8 and 9.

1.7 Perfect competition

We have mentioned in section 1.5 that the inverse of the demand elasticity can be used to indicate the degree of

monopoly power held in a market: the stiffer the competition
the higher the demand elasticity and the weaker the monopoly
power. Perfect competition can be regarded as a limiting case,
where competition is so intense that any individual supplier
has to accept the ruling market price because any attempt to
raise it will cause a complete loss of traffic; the elasticity is
infinite and the monopoly power is nil. Note from (1.6) that
this implies that a firm in perfect competition will adjust its
output to the point where its marginal cost is *equal* to the
given price. Hence a competitively supplied service will
generally be at a lower price and a greater quantity will be
consumed. We discuss the virtues of the idealized state of
perfect competition in chapter 5, the case for emulation of
it in the case of publicly owned enterprises in chapter 8 and
the reasons that the ideal may not be realized in practice in
chapter 9.

1.8 Consumer surplus

We now give the very simplest example of the way that the
demand curve can be used in the process of economic evaluation. A typical application is in the cost benefit analysis of
the question of whether it is worthwhile building some
facility such as a bridge, tunnel or road, or worthwhile paying
the subsidy necessary to keep some public transport facility
open. An important part of the problem is to decide what the
'best' price to charge would be in the sense of general com-
munity interest rather than profit.

The point where the demand curve cuts the vertical axis in
figure 1.2 is α. This is the amount that people would be
willing to pay for the first unit sold. Because of the slope of
the curve the willingness to pay for the second unit will be
somewhat less, given by the second shaded rectangle. By
extending this argument we may argue that the total *willingness to pay* for an amount q at price p is given by the sum of
the three areas A, B and C, i.e. $A + B + C$. The actual amount
that has to be paid is given by $B + C$ and so there is a surplus
benefit given by the area A. This is known as the 'consumer
surplus'. Sections 2.6 to 2.8 are devoted to more formal
demonstrations that changes in consumer surplus when prices
change can be related to changes in consumers' welfare.

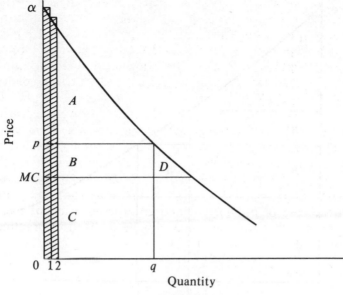

Figure 1.2

Suppose that marginal costs are independent of the level of output, as shown. Then the area C measures the total cost (ignoring any fixed costs) of producing the amount q. The area B is therefore operating profit. Suppose we now ask 'what is the best price to charge assuming the same price must be charged to all users?' Then we must choose a criterion of 'goodness'. A standard 'social cost benefit criterion' is *the willingness to pay net of production costs*:

$$(A + B + C) - C = A + B$$

This is known as the *net benefit*.

Now consider a small price reduction from p to p' in figure 1.3. There will be $(q' - q)$ extra users and their gross willingness to pay will be given by the area $D' + B'' + C'$. The cost of serving them will be C' and so there will be a net gain of $D' + B''$. The area B' is a simple transfer of what was previously a part of monopoly profit from the owners of the facility to the existing users. Whilst this affects the distribution of benefits, it can be ignored for the purposes of calculating net

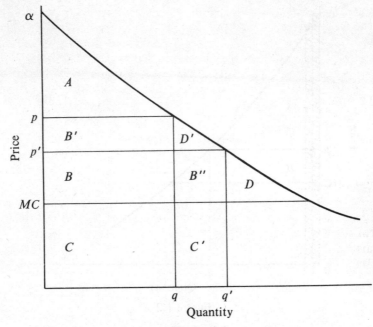

Figure 1.3

social benefits (see Layard 1972). B'' represents profit earned from the new users, and its ownership is irrelevant from the point of view of net social benefit. There is a remaining extra area D', which represents benefit to new users not extracted in the form of profit. The new net benefit $D' + B''$ is seen to be a part of D, which is known as the *economic deadloss* caused by pricing above marginal cost. Since net gains of this kind can always be generated by price reductions so long as price is above marginal cost, net benefits must be maximized when price is equal to marginal cost, and the economic deadloss is eliminated.

Calculation of triangles such as D is the essence of the estimation of welfare losses due to inefficient pricing caused by the presence of monopoly or some form of intervention. This is discussed at length in chapter 9.

The argument may be stated a little more formally as follows. The quantity sold is a function of the price charged:

$$q = f(p) \qquad (1.7)$$

The sum of the areas A, B and C net of production cost $c(q)$ is the net benefit:

$$\int_p^\alpha f(z)\,dz + pf(p) - c(q) \tag{1.8}$$

Differentiating with respect to price p and setting the derivative equal to zero,

$$-f(p) + f(p) - p\frac{df(p)}{dp} - \frac{dc}{dq}\frac{dq}{dp} = 0 \tag{1.9}$$

The first term in (1.9) comes from the fact that the derivative of an integral with respect to its lower limit is minus the value of the integrand evaluated at that lower limit. The last term results from using the chain rule for differentiation (see Glaister 1977, p. 113).

Bearing in mind that from (1.7)

$$\frac{df(p)}{dp} = \frac{dq}{dp}$$

(1.9) then immediately implies that

$$p = dc/dq$$

as before.

This *marginal cost pricing* prescription is fundamental and is a recurring result throughout the book. The reasons for this are developed in chapter 5. Note that it would be achieved by profit maximization in perfect competition and so there is a suggestion that a public enterprise should behave as if it were a competitive firm, although there are many complications to be added to this simplistic statement. Marginal cost pricing will not in general occur in the presence of monopoly or oligopoly and this is one reason for government intervention.

The rule implies a zero price where the marginal costs are zero as they might be in the case of an uncongested road or bridge. To charge a toll would then be to deny the use of the facility to some users who would otherwise have caused no costs to be incurred on their behalf. It follows that such a project should be financed from some source of general taxation rather than by attempting to recover the costs by direct charging, providing that alternative forms of taxation can be found which do not cause important violations of the optimality conditions elsewhere in the economy; these are discussed in chapter 4. The rule will also imply a loss if there are declining marginal costs (that is if there are increasing returns to scale). This provides one of the classic justifications for giving subsidies to railways, which is discussed in chapter 9. It does not allow price discrimination on the grounds of differing price elasticities. It does, however, imply variation of prices in line with variation of marginal costs if peaks occur.

In summary, chapter 2 discusses the way in which the demand for a service at given prices may be related to the preferences of individuals. It also shows how the demand curve may be used to estimate the changes in consumer welfare which are associated with changes in prices. Chapter 3 relates the supply of services to the objectives of the producer, the technology, the structure of costs and the structure of the industry. This chapter then brings the preceding material together to analyse the behaviour of markets. In chapter 4 the optimality of resource allocation is discussed and related to the outcome of competitive markets. The fundamental nature of the role of marginal cost is established. In chapter 5 the theory developed is applied to the problems of congestion, the peak, the 'second best', the 'public interest', pricing subject to loss constraints and income redistribution. Chapters 2 to 5 assume a deterministic world, but chapter 6 introduces some elementary queueing theory to illustrate how random variation can affect the arguments. Chapter 7 discusses modelling and estimation of transport demand. Chapter 8 discusses the way that all these considerations can be brought together in economic evaluation, investment decisions and public criteria. Chapter 9 concerns the economics of market intervention, regulation and the assessment of the costs and benefits of regulation.

2 Consumer Behaviour and the Demand Curve

This chapter is a concise account of those segments of the pure and applied study of the behaviour of the individual consumer which will be required in later chapters. The topic is at the core of the subject of this book. The aim of any applied economist is to improve understanding of the forces at work and to prescribe. His ultimate concern is with the felicity of the individuals in the society he is considering and with contributing towards the achievement of an improved compromise between their various interests, which, in the nature of things, must inevitably be in conflict.

We start by specifying a simple set of axioms on preferences which we require that a 'consistent' and 'rational' individual should satisfy in his behaviour in choosing between alternatives. We then describe how this allows the construction of a numerical function (i.e. the *utility function*) which provides a numerical ranking of alternatives which is equivalent to the underlying preference ordering. This rather remarkable result is convenient since it enables us to use the standard techniques of classical mathematical analysis. The assumption that one individual will behave so as to choose the alternative which he prefers from the multitude available to him leads to predictions about how the quantities of goods and services which he wishes to consume will respond to changes in their relative prices and his income (*the demand function*) — predictions which can be compared with observed market behaviour.

Conversely, and most importantly, we can relate changes in consumption in response to changes in relative prices and incomes to the consumer's preferences and hence to his welfare. The significance of this is that many matters the transport economist has to consider will involve just such changes in the prices and disposable incomes experienced by consumers. Examples are fares or taxation changes and infrastructure or vehicle investments. The study of 'consumer surplus', which is a technique for attributing a valuation of such changes to the consumer, is an important component in current applied transport economics practice. Finally we have to face the difficulties encountered in *aggregation* − in practice one is almost invariably dealing with the result of group behaviour rather than that of the individual.

This standard body of economic theory is not put forward in the naive belief that individuals actually behave according to its letter in the 'real world'. Rather it is an attempt to provide a logically consistent model of preferences and implied behaviour as a guide or skeleton upon which to hang any constructive discussion of a practical problem. After all, the transport economist can only make a scientific contribution if there is at least a germ of consistency and radionality in behaviour. Any theory describing such behaviour must necessarily look similar to the one we are about to describe.

Before starting a formal account we must warn that we are deliberately glossing over some of the finer technical difficulties in the interests of clarity and continuity. There are many texts giving a more complete account: Malinvaud (1972) and Deaton and Muellbauer (1980) are excellent ones. Not all the results of sections 2.3, 2.4 and 2.5 are explicitly used in the rest of this book. They are included so as to provide a sound and complete basis for the consumer welfare analysis which follows. The important results are the relationship between consumer preferences and the utility function, the derivation of the demand functions (2.4) from the consumer's choice problem (2.1), the absence of money illusion, the distinction between the substitution and income effects in the Slutsky equation (2.22), Roy's identity (2.27), and especially the compensated demand function (2.30) and its derivation from (2.28), the expenditure function (2.31).

2.1 Consumer preferences

Let us suppose that in unit time an individual consumes quantities of goods and services given by x_i, $i = 1, 2, \ldots, n$. These will normally be non-negative numbers but by convention anything which he produces rather than consumes will be a negative number. Labour (say x_n) is the most obvious example of this. Let x denote the column vector $(x_1, x_2, \ldots, x_n)'$ and let x^1 and x^2 be two alternative vectors the individual might choose. Then we write $x^1 \geqslant x^2$ to mean 'x^1 is preferred or indifferent to x^2' and specify the following axioms for any individual's preferences:

> *A1* (Completeness). For any two vectors available to the individual either $x^1 \geqslant x^2$ or $x^2 \geqslant x^1$ or both.

This simply guarantees that he will be able to come to a decision one way or the other. Inability to do so is not permitted. If both relations hold then he is indifferent between the vectors.

> *A2* (Transitivity). If $x^1 \geqslant x^2$ and also $x^2 \geqslant x^3$ then $x^1 \geqslant x^3$.

This is a most elementary consistency requirement. Without it it is clear that no coherent theory could be developed.

> *A3* (Reflexivity). It is always the case that $x^1 \geqslant x^1$.

This ensures the option of indifference between vectors.

> *A4* (Continuity). The sets $\{x \mid x \geqslant x^1\}$ and $\{x \mid x^1 \geqslant x\}$ are closed.

This is a somewhat more technical restriction which ensures a degree of continuity or smoothness in behaviour.

Given these axioms Debreu (1959) has proved the following fundamental result: there exists a function $u(x)$ with the property that,

$$u(x^1) \geqslant u(x^2) \quad \text{if and only if} \quad x^1 \geqslant x^2$$

This function is known as a utility function. It has the property that if one collection of goods, x^1, is preferred or indifferent to another, x^2, then it registers a higher value. Whilst the preference system defined by the axioms is in some senses more elemental, the utility function is entirely equivalent to it and is much more amenable to analysis.

It follows directly from the definition that any order-preserving transform of a utility function (like multiplying it by a positive number) is another utility function representing *the same* set of preferences. The actual numerical values taken by the function are therefore irrelevant: it is the ranking which matters. For this reason we say that the function provides an *ordinal* (as opposed to cardinal) representation of preferences.

Throughout most of this book we shall assume that all the quantities are continuously variable and that the utility function is differentiable, although we do discuss the problem of discrete choice in chapter 7. The first partial derivatives of the utility function are denoted by

$$\partial u/\partial x_i \quad i = 1, 2, \ldots, n$$

These are known as the *marginal utilities*, being the extra utility gained by the consumption of one extra unit of x_i, holding the quantities of the other goods constant. We shall make the weak additional assumption that these marginal utilities are strictly positive, so that the consumer is always better off if he consumes more of any one good (or does less work) and the same quantities of the other goods. This is known as the assumption of *non-satiation*.

2.2 The 'standard' consumer analysis

Let $p = (p_1, p_2, \ldots, p_n)$ be a row vector of the prices faced by the consumer. These are assumed to be non-negative and constant. If good n represents labour then p_n would be the wage rate. Also, let m represent unearned income. Then we hypothesize that the individual chooses the quantities $x_1, x_2, \ldots, x_n$ so as to maximize his satisfaction within the total expenditure available to him. In other words his problem is to

$$\text{maximize } u(x) \text{ subject to } p \cdot x \leqslant m \tag{2.1}$$

Because of the assumption of non-satiation we can safely assume that at the solution the constraint will be binding, and so it can be written as

$$\mathbf{p} \cdot \mathbf{x} = \sum_{i=1}^{n} p_i x_i = \sum_{i=1}^{n-1} p_i x_i + p_n x_n = m \tag{2.2}$$

The Lagrangian for this problem is given by

$$L(\mathbf{x}, \lambda) = u(\mathbf{x}) - \lambda(\mathbf{p} \cdot \mathbf{x} - m)$$

and the first-order conditions are

$$\partial u / \partial x_i = \lambda p_i \quad i = 1, 2, \ldots, n \tag{2.3}$$

and $\mathbf{p} \cdot \mathbf{x} = m$.

The solution to these conditions may be written

$$x_i = f_i(\mathbf{p}, m) \quad i = 1, 2, \ldots, n \tag{2.4}$$

Before recording the properties of the demand functions (2.4) it is important to interpret the fundamental conditions (2.3). Taking the ratio of any two of them yields

$$\frac{\partial u / \partial x_j}{\partial u / \partial x_i} = \frac{p_j}{p_i} \tag{2.5}$$

The quantity on the left is known as the marginal rate of substitution of good i for good j, and is the number of units of good i which the individual requires to compensate him for a unit loss of good j. This is seen as follows. Suppose that utility is held constant at some arbitrary level $\bar{u}$:

$$u(\mathbf{x}) = \bar{u} \tag{2.6}$$

Differentiating with respect to x_j, allowing only x_i and x_j to vary, gives

$$\frac{\partial u}{\partial x_i} \frac{dx_i}{dx_j} + \frac{\partial u}{\partial x_j} = 0 \tag{2.7}$$

and so

$$-\frac{dx_i}{dx_j} = \frac{\partial u / \partial x_j}{\partial u / \partial x_i} \tag{2.8}$$

We can now see why (2.5) is necessary for a maximum for every pair of goods: if, say, the left were less than the right the individual could forgo one unit of j, trade it for p_j / p_i

units of i and achieve a net increase in utility, without any increase in money income. A maximum could therefore not have been attained.

Note that (2.5) still holds in the special case that good i is labour. It then says that the marginal rate of substitution of labour for any good j should equal the price of the good relative to the wage rate; that is, the number of hours work required in order to earn sufficient to purchase one unit of the good. Bear in mind that labour, being a 'good' offered rather than consumed, is measured as a negative number, $x_n < 0$. Thus an increase in x_n means a *fall* in the absolute value of x_n, which would represent a fall in the number of hours worked. Equation (2.3) implies that all marginal utilities must be positive, which in the case of labour corresponds to the notion that if all other goods are held constant, less labour will correspond to a higher level of utility.

There is one extra restriction which must be placed on the utility function in order that we may be sure that the solutions (2.4) to the conditions (2.3) are unique and global maxima. The assumption is known as 'strict quasi-concavity'. Amongst other things it requires that the marginal utility of any good be diminishing:

$$\partial^2 u / \partial x_i^2 \leqslant 0$$

as one has more and more of any good the extra utility derived from an extra unit declines. It also implies that the marginal rate of substitution between any two goods in (2.5) must be diminishing; as one has more and more of a good, fewer and fewer units of another good are required in order to compensate for the loss of one unit of the first good (see Glaister 1977, chapter 17 for more detail).

2.3 Properties of demand functions

A more leisurely account of the material of this section will be found in Henderson and Quandt (1971) or Glaister (1977).

(1) The first property concerns the Lagrangian multiplier. Being the 'shadow price' on the income constraint λ has the usual interpretation as the increase in the objective function

attainable given a unit relaxation of the constraint. In this case it is the *marginal utility of income*. To demonstrate this multiply each condition in (2.3) by $\partial x_i / \partial m$ and add:

$$\sum_{i=1}^{n} \frac{\partial u}{\partial x_i} \frac{\partial x_i}{\partial m} = \lambda \sum_{i=1}^{n} p_i \frac{\partial x_i}{\partial m}$$

But, by differentiating (2.2)

$$\sum_{i=1}^{n} p_i \frac{\partial x_i}{\partial m} = 1$$

hence

$$\partial u / \partial m = \lambda \qquad (2.9)$$

which proves the result. It follows that, as we shall see, λ is a very important quantity in applied welfare economics because many actions implicitly involve the transfer of money income from one individual (say 'the rich') to another (say 'the poor') and one is interested in the net change in total welfare. The marginal utility of income measures the utility change of each individual. However, to give a cardinal significance to marginal utility – and hence utility – so that the changes can be added or subtracted is to go further than many economists would be willing to go.

(2) An equiproportionate change in all prices (including the wage rate) and unearned money income will not alter the constraint (2.2) and so it cannot alter the demands in (2.4): the demand functions are 'homogeneous of degree zero in price and income'. This is known as the *absence of money illusion* and is the first testable prediction from the theory.

Euler's theorem for a function $g(\mathbf{x})$, homogeneous of degree r states that

$$\sum_{j} \frac{\partial g}{\partial x_j} x_j = rg(\mathbf{x})$$

For (2.4) this implies that

$$\sum_{j} \frac{\partial x_i}{\partial p_j} p_j + \frac{\partial x_i}{\partial m} m = 0, \qquad (2.10)$$

or after multiplying by $1/x_i$ to convert it into elasticity terms

$$\sum_j \eta_{ij} + \eta_{im} = 0 \quad i = 1, 2, \dots, n \qquad (2.11)$$

This is a useful relationship between the sum of the cross-price elasticities and the income elasticity of each good.

(3) The next properties are obtained from a 'comparative static' analysis of the relations (2.2). That is, a static analysis of changes in the demand equilibrium implied by (2.2) in response to local variations in all the independent variables, denoted by dp_i and dm. It is known as the *compensated* response of demand for good i with respect to a change in price j. From (2.2) we obtain

$$\begin{bmatrix} U & p' \\ p & 0 \end{bmatrix} \begin{bmatrix} dx \\ -d\lambda \end{bmatrix} = \begin{bmatrix} \lambda I & 0 \\ -x' & 1 \end{bmatrix} \begin{bmatrix} dp' \\ dm \end{bmatrix} \qquad (2.12)$$

where U is the symmetric matrix whose elements are $\partial^2 u / \partial x_i \, \partial x_j$. 'Solving' for $(dx, -d\lambda)'$ gives

$$\begin{bmatrix} dx \\ -d\lambda \end{bmatrix} = \begin{bmatrix} V & w \\ w' & z \end{bmatrix} \begin{bmatrix} \lambda I & 0 \\ -x' & 1 \end{bmatrix} \begin{bmatrix} dp' \\ dm \end{bmatrix} \qquad (2.13)$$

where the first matrix on the right-hand side of (2.13) is the inverse of the left-hand matrix of (2.12); V is a symmetric matrix (because of the symmetry of U), w is a column vector and z is a scalar. This yields

$$dx = (\lambda V - w . x') \, dp' + w \, dm$$

$$= \lambda V \, dp' - w . x' \, dp' + w \, dm \qquad (2.14)$$

In order to aid the interpretation of (2.14) consider the differential of the constraint (2.2):

$$p . dx + x' . dp' = dm \qquad (2.15)$$

But if utility is constant, we have from (2.7)

$$\sum_i \frac{\partial u}{\partial x_i} \, dx_i = 0 \qquad (2.16)$$

and from (2.4) this implies that

$$\lambda \mathbf{p} . d\mathbf{x} = 0 \tag{2.17}$$

Hence under these circumstances (2.15) implies that

$$\mathbf{x}' . d\mathbf{p}' = dm$$

It follows from (2.14) that if $d\mathbf{p}$ and dm are arranged in such a way as to hold utility constant then

$$d\mathbf{x} = \lambda \mathbf{V} d\mathbf{p}' \tag{2.18}$$

or if the elements of $\mathbf{V}$ are denoted v_{ij},

$$\frac{\delta x_i}{\delta p_j} = \lambda v_{ij} \quad i, j = 1, 2, \ldots, n \tag{2.19}$$

The notation $\delta x_i / \delta p_j$ is a special one to indicate that it is the change in demand for good i in response to a change in price of good j holding all other prices constant, but making a compensating change in income *so as to hold utility constant*.

On the other hand, taking the special case $d\mathbf{p} = 0$ we have

$$d\mathbf{x} = \mathbf{w} \, dm \tag{2.20}$$

or

$$\partial x_i / \partial m = w_i \tag{2.21}$$

Thus when only price j changes and income is held constant, i.e. $dm = 0$, (2.14) becomes

$$\frac{\partial x_i}{\partial p_j} = \frac{\delta x_i}{\delta p_j} - x_j \frac{\partial x_i}{\partial m} \quad i, j = 1, 2, \ldots, n \tag{2.22}$$

This fundamental equation is known as Slutsky's equation. In elasticity form it can be written

$$\eta_{ij} = (\eta_{ij})^c - \gamma_j \eta_{im} \tag{2.23}$$

where $\gamma_j = p_j x_j / m$ is the proportion of income expended on good j, and $(\eta_{ij})^c$ denotes the compensated cross-price elasticity.

(4) Taking now the case $i = j$ in (2.22) we have

$$\frac{\partial x_i}{\partial p_i} = \frac{\delta x_i}{\delta p_i} - x_i \frac{\partial x_i}{\partial m} \qquad (2.24)$$

The strict quasi-concavity of the utility function implies that the matrix $\mathbf{U}$ and hence the matrix $\mathbf{V}$ are negative definite. It follows that the compensated price effect in (2.24), known as *the substitution effect*, is negative. Hence so long as the income effect is positive we predict that the overall impact of a price increase is to reduce demand: *the demand curve slopes downwards*. There are examples of goods which have negative income effects, known as inferior goods. Public transport may be one because as people become richer they become more likely to own cars (see chapter 7) and so their use of the public transport alternative falls. There are, however, very few examples (and none in transport) for which the negative income effect has been shown to outweigh the substitution effect so as to give an upward sloping demand curve.

The interpretation of the split in (2.24) of a price effect into a substitution and an income effect is important. Clearly, if the price of a good increases and income is increased simultaneously so as to hold attainable utility constant, then there will always be a tendency to substitute other goods for it. Further, if money income is held constant then the individual's real income has fallen because a price has risen, so there will normally be tendency to consume less of it on that count as well.

(5) The symmetry of $\mathbf{U}$ follows from the symmetry of cross partial derivatives and through (2.19) in turn implies that the substitution effects are symmetrical:

$$\frac{\delta x_i}{\delta p_j} = \frac{\partial x_i}{\partial p_j} + x_j \frac{\partial x_i}{\partial m} = \frac{\partial x_j}{\partial p_i} + x_i \frac{\partial x_j}{\partial m} = \frac{\delta x_j}{\delta p_i} \qquad (2.25)$$

This rather remarkable result provides a further prediction against which the theory may be tested. We shall see that this is one of several reasons for preferring to work with *compensated* effects in much theoretical work.

(6) As a matter of definition, if $\delta x_i/\delta p_j > 0$ then goods i and j are said to be substitutes, because a rise in price j will be associated with a fall in consumption of j and a simultaneous increase in consumption of good i. Otherwise they are said to be complements.

2.4 The indirect utility function

Having solved for the demand functions $x_i = f_i(\mathbf{p}, m)$, it is a simple matter to replace the x_i in $u(\mathbf{x})$ with the solution values to give a new function $h(\mathbf{p}, m)$ which is known as the *indirect utility function*. It expresses the maximum utility attainable with income m at prices $\mathbf{p}$. Fairly obviously

$$\lambda = \text{marginal utility of income} = h_m(\mathbf{p}, m) = \frac{\partial h(\mathbf{p}, m)}{\partial m}$$

(2.26)

It is also true that

$$x_i = -\frac{\partial h(\mathbf{p}, m)/\partial p_i}{\partial h(\mathbf{p}, m)/\partial m} \quad i = 1, 2, \ldots, n \qquad (2.27)$$

This most useful result means that the demand functions can be constructed from a knowledge of the indirect utility function in a very simple manner. The result is important in the interpretation of consumer surplus (see below): it is known as Roy's identity.

2.5 The dual approach: the expenditure function

The problem was originally expressed as maximizing utility subject to an expenditure constraint. The dual problem is to minimize expenditure subject to a utility constraint: that is, to find the cheapest way of attaining a prespecified level of utility:

$$\text{minimize } \mathbf{p} \cdot \mathbf{x} \text{ subject to } u(\mathbf{x}) = \bar{u} \qquad (2.28)$$

If μ is the Lagrangian multiplier for the problem then the first-order conditions are

$$p_i = \mu \frac{\partial u}{\partial x_i} \quad i = 1, 2, \ldots, n$$

and

$$u(\mathbf{x}) = \bar{u} \tag{2.29}$$

which are very similar to those obtained in (2.3). The quasi-concavity of the utility function again provides the sufficiency conditions. Conditions (2.29) may be solved to give the *compensated demand functions*,

$$x_i^c = f_i^c(\mathbf{p}, \bar{u}) \tag{2.30}$$

Substituting these in the objective gives the *expenditure function*,

$$g(\mathbf{p}, \bar{u}) = \sum_i p_i x_i^c \tag{2.31}$$

This measures the minimum amount of money that this individual requires to allow him to reach the specified utility level.

It is easy to show that the expenditure function has the following properties:

(1) $g(\mathbf{p}, \bar{u})$ is homogeneous of degree one in prices. For example, doubling all prices will double the minimum expenditure required to attain the given level of utility.

(2)
$$\frac{\partial g}{\partial p_i} = f_i^c(\mathbf{p}, \bar{u}) \quad i = 1, 2, \ldots, n \tag{2.32}$$

so that, analogously with the indirect utility function, a knowledge of the expenditure function allows calculation of the compensated demand function in a very simple manner.

(3) From (2.32) it follows that

$$\frac{\partial f_i^c}{\partial p_j} = \frac{\partial^2 g}{\partial p_j \partial p_i} = \frac{\partial^2 g}{\partial p_i \partial p_j} = \frac{\partial f_j^c}{\partial p_i}$$

which is a simple confirmation of the symmetry of the pure substitution effect, shown in (2.25).

Suppose that the given income m is such that the utility attainable in the solution of the primal problem (2.1) is the same as the given utility in the dual problem (2.8). Then the solutions (2.4) and (2.30) to the two problems must be the same:

$$f_i(\mathbf{p}, m) = f_i^c(\mathbf{p}, \bar{u}) \quad i = 1, 2, \ldots, n$$

Differentiating with respect to p_j

$$\frac{\partial f_i}{\partial p_j} + \frac{\partial f_i}{\partial m} \frac{\partial m}{\partial p_j} = \frac{\partial f_i^c}{\partial p_j}$$

and using (2.31) and (2.32) gives

$$\frac{\partial f_i}{\partial p_j} = \frac{\partial f_i^c}{\partial p_j} - f_j \frac{\partial f_i}{\partial m} \quad i, j = 1, 2, \ldots, n$$

This is just Slutsky's equation (2.22) and the argument we have just given is an alternative derivation of it.

2.6 Consumer surplus

This topic has become important relatively recently in applied transport economics. The idea, suggested by Dupuit (1844), Marshall (1920) and many others, as a measure of consumer welfare changes, is a very simple and appealing one. However, it has become the subject of a large and somewhat confusing body of theoretical literature: Currie, Murphy and Schmitz (1971) and Seade (1978) give surveys. In what follows we aim to give a much simplified account of the relationship between consumer surplus and standard choice theory, which avoids many of the complexities of a fully rigorous analysis. We would emphasize that whilst consumer surplus is used as a convenient method of exposition in following chapters it is not essential to the argument; the results can be obtained in other ways.

A mathematical description of the notion of consumer surplus which corresponds to figure 1.2 is as follows. Suppose unearned income and all prices except p_1 remain constant and consider a fall in p_1 from p_1^0 to p_1. We may abbreviate the demand function for good 1 to

$$x_1 = f_1(p_1) \tag{2.33}$$

with

$$f_1'(p_1) = df_1/dp_1 < 0 \tag{2.34}$$

Now, at price p_1^0 the consumer would like to buy $x_1^0 = f_1(p_1^0)$ units. If the price falls by the infinitesimal, dp_1, then each of the x_1^0 units becomes that much cheaper and there is a benefit of $x_1^0 dp_1$ because this is the fall in expenditure required to obtain x_1^0. The calculation of the benefit from the next incremental fall in price would have to take into account the increase in demand caused by the first fall. The total benefit of a fall from p_1^0 to p_1 would be given by the integral

$$\int_{p_1}^{p_1^0} f_1(z) \, dz \tag{2.35}$$

where z is the dummy variable of the integration. To put this another way, the individual would be willing to pay p_1^0 for the first x_1^0 units but, after the price fall, he actually only has to pay p_1 for those units. A similar argument applies to each intramarginal unit of x_1, and the total benefit attributable to the price fall again reduces to the 'area' given in (2.35) and labelled as $B + D$ in figure 1.2. In the special case where $p_1^0 = \alpha_1$, say, the price at which none of the good would be demanded, then (2.35) becomes the *consumer surplus* attributable to good 1 at price p_1 (area A in figure 1.2). Also

$$\int_{p_1}^{\alpha_1} f_1(z) \, dz + p_1 f(p_1) \tag{2.36}$$

is known as the total 'willingness to pay' for good 1 at price p_1 (areas $A + B + C$ of figure 1.2), the second term of (2.36) being simply the expenditure on good 1.

One way of relating consumer surplus changes as in (2.35) to individual welfare changes as defined previously is through Roy's identity (2.27). Using this (2.35) becomes

$$-\int_{p_1}^{p_1^0} \left(\frac{\partial h(\mathbf{p}, m)/\partial p_1}{\partial h(\mathbf{p}, m)/\partial m} \right) dp_1$$

where the indirect utility function $h(\mathbf{p}, m)$ represents the maximum utility attainable at prices $\mathbf{p}$ and income m. If the marginal utility of income $\partial h/\partial m$ (or λ) is independent of p_1

then this can be written

$$-\frac{1}{\lambda}\int_{p_1}^{p_1^0} \frac{\partial h(\mathbf{p}, m)}{\partial p_1} \, dp_1$$

$$=\frac{1}{\lambda}[h(p_1, p_2, \ldots, p_n, m) - h(p_1^0, p_2, \ldots, p_n, m)]$$

$$(2.37)$$

This is simply the gain in utility caused by the fall in price of good 1, converted into money terms by dividing by the marginal utility of income. Note that the validity of this result does depend upon the assumption that the marginal utility of income is independent of the price in question.

A second justification of the consumer surplus measure is found if the demand function in (2.35) is taken to be the compensated demand function of (2.30). Then (2.35) with (2.31) gives

$$\int_{p_1}^{p_1^0} f_1^c(\mathbf{p}, \bar{u}) \, dp_1$$

$$=\int_{p_1}^{p_1^0} \frac{\partial g(\mathbf{p}, \bar{u})}{\partial p_1} \, dp_1$$

$$= g(p_1^0, p_2, -p_n, \bar{u}) - g(p_1, p_2, \ldots, p_n, \bar{u}) \quad (2.38)$$

Hence on this interpretation of the demand function, the consumer surplus is simply the change in expenditure required to allow the individual to maintain a constant level of utility as the price changes. This is a most important concept in welfare economics and is known as the *compensating variation*. It is an ideal cost of living index. The compensating variation is the measure used in most applications in this book, although there are in fact several alternative measures of consumer surplus. The intricate arguments discussing their merits are set out in Deaton and Muellbauer (1980).

2.7 The multiple price change case

In general a policy will involve changing more than one price. Then the *vector* $\mathbf{p}^0$ would change to $\mathbf{p}$, some components remaining constant in general. The generalization of (2.25) is then the line integral (as first proposed by Hotelling 1938):

$$\int_{\gamma} \mathbf{f}^{c}(\mathbf{p}, \bar{u}) \cdot d\mathbf{p} \tag{2.39}$$

where γ is the path of integration and $\mathbf{f}^{c}(\mathbf{p}, \bar{u})$ is the vector of compensated demand functions. The value of (2.39) will not depend upon the path of integration because $\mathbf{f}^{c}(\mathbf{p}, \bar{u})$ is the gradient of a potential function (see Apostol 1957), namely the expenditure function, and hence, as we have shown in (2.25), the required condition of symmetry on the first derivatives of $\mathbf{f}^{c}(\mathbf{p}, \bar{u})$ is satisfied.

Thus any path will suffice and a convenient one is

$$(p_1^0, p_2^0, \ldots, p_n^0) \to (p_1, p_2^0, \ldots, p_n^0) \to (p_1, p_2, \ldots, p_n^0)$$

$$\to (p_1, p_2, \ldots, p_n) \tag{2.40}$$

With this path (2.38) becomes

$$\int_{p_1}^{p_1^0} f_1^c(z, p_2^0, \ldots, p_n^0, \bar{u}) \, dz$$

$$+ \int_{p_2}^{p_2^0} f_2^c(p_1, z, \ldots, p_n^0, \bar{u}) \, dz$$

$$+ \ldots + \int_{p_n}^{p_n^0} f_n^c(p_1, p_2, \ldots, z, \bar{u}) \, dz$$

$$= g(p_1^0, p_2^0, \ldots, p_n^0, \bar{u}) - g(p_1, p_2, \ldots, p_n, \bar{u}) \tag{2.41}$$

The method of evaluation embodied in (2.41) is to be found in many texts (for instance, Hicks 1956). It may be described as evaluating the surplus for good 1 holding other prices at their old levels, evaluating the surplus for good 2 holding price of good 1 at its new level and other prices at their old levels, and so on. The sum in (2.41) then gives the total compensating variation.

A parallel argument may easily be constructed involving the indirect utility function if the demand function is the 'normal' one, $f_1(\mathbf{p}, m)$. Note, however, that in this case validity depends upon the independence of the marginal utility of income from each of the prices which changes. This may give rise to logical difficulties (see Samuelson 1942 or Green 1971). However, there are several reasons for preferring to work with the compensated demand function (see Friedman 1949). As (2.23) suggests, the difference between the compensated and 'normal' elasticities is related to the income elasticity. The difference will be small if the product of the latter and the proportion of income spent on the goods in question is small. In practice this is often the case, and so it is convenient to accept the traditional consumer surplus measure as a good approximation to the compensating variation.

2.8 Aggregation

The discussion so far has been entirely in terms of the areas under the demand curves of individuals. In practice the demand curves that are observed and used in evaluation of policies are market demand curves comprising the results of actions by many individuals. Let X_i denote the total demand for good i where,

$$X_i = \sum_{h=1}^{H} x_i^h \qquad (2.42)$$

and x_i^h is the demand by individual h. Then

$$\int_{P_1}^{p_1^0} X_i \, dz = \int_{P_1}^{p_1^0} \left(\sum_{h=1}^{H} x_i^h \right) dz$$

$$= \sum_{h=1}^{H} \int_{P_1}^{p_1^0} x_i^h \, dz \qquad (2.43)$$

This establishes that the area under an aggregate demand curve can be thought of as a sum of areas under individual demand curves. Each of the latter can be given either the indirect utility interpretation of (2.37) or the compensating variation interpretation of (2.38).

It is important to note that one implication of using (2.43) as a measure of total welfare change under either interpretation is that it will make no difference to the result if, at the same time as the price change, there is a transfer of money from any one individual to any other. The measure is thus neutral with respect to changes in the distribution of income between individuals. It can only be strictly correct to assume this if we believe that the present distribution of income is 'optimum'; otherwise some lump sum transfers would necessarily increase or decrease social welfare. Ways in which the measure (2.43) may be modified to take account of non-neutral views on the current distribution of income are illustrated in section 8.4.

The whole of this chapter has been written on the assumption that each individual varies his demand for each good continuously. Chapter 7 gives a parallel derivation of the connection between individual welfare and the area under aggregate demand curves in cases where individuals face discrete choices — no car or one car, for instance. Movement along a demand curve then occurs as a few individuals change their choices whilst the majority do not change their behaviour.

2.9 The evaluation of service quality changes

Very often the management of a public enterprise, such as an urban bus service, has to make decisions about not only what prices to charge, but also what quality of service to offer. An illustration of the way that the analysis of section 2.7 can be extended to deal with this problem follows (Bruzelius 1979, gives a similar argument).

Let x_1 and x_2 be the quantities of two transport goods consumed at money prices p_1 and p_2 (say in passenger miles per annum). Let y be a (scalar) 'composite' of all other goods whose relative prices are to be regarded as constant. Prices may be scaled so that the composite has a unit price. For the sake of the argument we shall identify 'quality' with the time it takes to make a unit trip. This will be determined both by the speed at which the vehicle travels and, in the case of a non-timetabled service, by the frequency of service that is offered. Let q_i be the time taken to consume a unit of the transport good x_i, T be the maximum time available for consumption and leisure activities and l be the time the consumer chooses to take as leisure. For simplicity of exposition we assume that the time required for work is fixed. Thus the problem may be formulated as (the generalization to more than two modes is immediate)

$$\text{minimize} \quad y + p_1 x_1 + p_2 x_2$$

$$\text{subject to} \quad u(y, x_1, x_2, l) \geqslant u \tag{2.44}$$

$$\text{and} \quad q_1 x_1 + q_2 x_2 + l = T$$

Solving this gives the compensated demand functions

$$y(\mathbf{p}, \mathbf{q}, u) \quad \text{and} \quad x_i(\mathbf{p}, \mathbf{q}, u) \tag{2.45}$$

and the expenditure function

$$g(\mathbf{p}, \mathbf{q}, u) = y(\mathbf{p}, \mathbf{q}, u) + p_1 x_1(\mathbf{p}, \mathbf{q}, u) + p_2 x_2(\mathbf{p}, \mathbf{q}, u) \tag{2.46}$$

This is directly comparable with (2.31) and, as in (2.38), the change in it when prices or quantities change is the amount of money which has to be given to or taken from the individual in order for him to remain as well as he was before the change, i.e. the compensating variation. Property (2.32) still holds:

$$\frac{\partial g(\mathbf{p}, \mathbf{q}, u)}{\partial p_i} = x_i(\mathbf{p}, \mathbf{q}, u) \tag{2.47}$$

In addition, the rate of change with respect to the time required to travel a passenger mile is the demand for the respective good multiplied by the value of time τ:

$$\frac{\partial g(\mathbf{p}, \mathbf{q}, u)}{\partial q_i} = \tau x_i(\mathbf{p}, \mathbf{q}, u) \tag{2.48}$$

Bruzelius (1979) provides a proof.

Here τ is the shadow price on the overall time constraint in the minimization problem. It measures the increase in money expenditure which would be required to enable the individual to maintain his level of utility if one less unit of time were available to him in total.

Suppose that a proposal which involves a change of (p'_1, p'_2, q'_1, q'_2) to $(p''_1, p''_2, q''_1, q''_2)$ is to be evaluated. That is, both money and time costs are to be altered simultaneously in two interdependent markets. The compensating variation is

$$g(\mathbf{p''}, \mathbf{q''}, u) - g(\mathbf{p'}, \mathbf{q'}, u)$$
$$= g(\mathbf{p''}, \mathbf{q''}, u) - g(\mathbf{p'}, \mathbf{q''}, u) + g(\mathbf{p'}, \mathbf{q''}, u) - g(\mathbf{p'}, \mathbf{q'}, u)$$
$$(2.49)$$

The first pair of terms here represents the compensating variation as the prices change holding times at their new values and the second pair is the compensating variation as the times change, holding prices at their old values. Now consider two line integrals:

$$\int_{\gamma_1} [x_1(z, \mathbf{q''}, u)\, dz_1 + x_2(z, \mathbf{q}, u)\, dz_2]$$

$$+ \int_{\gamma_2} [\tau x_1(\mathbf{p'}, z, u)\, dz_1 + \tau x_2(\mathbf{p'}, z, u)\, dz_2] \qquad (2.50)$$

Because of the cross-price symmetry and cross-time symmetry properties of compensated demand functions (demonstrated in (2.25)) these line integrals are independent of the path. For convenience we may take the paths

$$(p'_1, p'_2, q''_1, q''_2) \rightarrow (p''_1, p'_2, q''_1, q''_2) \rightarrow (p''_1, p''_2, q''_1, q''_2)$$

and

$$(p'_1, p'_2, q'_1, q'_2) \rightarrow (p'_1, p'_2, q''_1, q'_2) \rightarrow (p'_1, p'_2, q''_1, q''_2)$$

Expression (2.50) then becomes

$$\int_{p'_1}^{p''_1} x_1(z, p'_2, q''_2, u)\, dz + \int_{p'_2}^{p''_2} x_2(p''_1, z, q''_1, q''_2, u)\, dz$$

$$+ \int_{q'_1}^{q''_1} \tau x_1(p'_1, p'_2, z, q'_2)\, dz + \int_{q'_2}^{q''_2} \tau x_2(p'_1, p'_2, q''_1, z)\, dz$$

$$(2.51)$$

Because of the properties of the partial derivatives of the expenditure function, (2.47) and (2.48), this is the same as compensating variation in (2.49).

Each term in (2.51) corresponds to a change in the area under a demand curve as a respective price or time varies, holding other prices and times constant at the specified values. We apply this analysis in section 8.5 on the problem of service quality.

3 The Producer

This chapter describes some of the mechanisms by which goods and services are supplied. In some cases this may be done by a myriad of small organizations working in competition with each other — some sectors of the road haulage industry and minicab firms are examples. In other cases a rather smaller number of suppliers may compete as in the domestic US airline industry or they may be organized into cooperative cartels as in shipping and international airline industries. Finally, there may be a single provider who is often more or less under central government control. Examples of such public enterprises are the railways, most bus services and trunk road building and maintenance which is carried out by central government directly.

Almost without exception the consideration of any matter concerning any of these suppliers will require an assessment of two central components: revenue and cost. Or, more specifically, it will require an assessment of what will happen to these components as the result of some proposed action, i.e. *marginal revenues* and *marginal* (or *avoidable*) *costs*.

3.1 Revenue

Suppose we are considering a specific good and the producer is able to assume all prices other than his own selling price to be constant. We may denote the aggregate demand (suppressing the subscript for clarity) by

$$x = f(p) \qquad (3.1)$$

This expresses the number of units that can be sold at the stated price in unit time. The function $f(p)$ is continuous and monotonic decreasing on the usual assumptions as stated in the previous chapter. Hence the function may be inverted to give

$$p = g(x) = f^{-1}(x) \qquad (3.2)$$

which gives the price at which any specified number of units may be sold. The derivatives of the two versions of the demand function will be mutual inverses:

$$\frac{dg(x)}{dx} = \left(\frac{df(p)}{dp}\right)^{-1} \qquad (3.3)$$

Total revenue may be expressed either as a function of price or of quantity, but the latter is more convenient for the present purpose:

$$R(x) = xg(x) \qquad (3.4)$$

Then consider the rate of change of revenue with respect to a change in units sold, the so called *marginal revenue*:

$$\frac{dR(x)}{dx} = x\frac{dg(x)}{dx} + g(x)$$

$$= g(x)\left(\frac{x}{g(x)}\frac{dg(x)}{dx} + 1\right)$$

$$= p\left(1 + \frac{1}{\eta}\right) \qquad (3.5)$$

where

$$\eta = \frac{p}{f(p)}\frac{df(p)}{dp} = \frac{g(x)}{x}\left(\frac{dg(x)}{dx}\right)^{-1}$$

is the elasticity of demand, defined in chapter 1.

Equation (3.5) embodies a simple but fundamental rule. If $-1 < \eta < 0$ then the marginal revenue will be negative and vice versa. Hence we see that if the demand is inelastic (that is, if $|\eta| < 1$ so that an increase in price will cause a relatively small reduction in demand) then a price increase (quantity reduction) will generate an increased revenue. On the other hand if the demand is elastic then a price increase will cause a *reduction* in revenue. It follows that a knowledge of the demand elasticity is essential to any operator who wishes to vary his revenue by price variation, and it is by no means obvious that the way to increase revenue is to increase price — especially in cases where the service in question has close competitors which would tend to make it sensitive to price.

This relatively simple fact is a frequent source of much confusion as is illustrated by the continuing debate between the public, management and unions about whether British Rail fares should be raised or lowered in order to reduce the operating deficit. It happens that current evidence on rail demand elasticities is inconclusive, but such as it is it would indicate that whilst elasticities on short distance commuting routes may well be significantly less than unity, those on longer intercity routes may be close to, or in some cases significantly above unity.

It will be noted that the foregoing discussion has been in terms of marginal changes in the strict sense, and that the elasticities referred to were point elasticities. There is no general presumption that elasticities will be constant as prices increase over a non-marginal range. Indeed one would generally expect changes to occur, but in much practical empirical work the range of experience is limited and the data are of limited quality so that it is extremely difficult to measure demand characteristics. For this reason the *constant* elasticity function is frequently fitted to data, on the grounds that it is log-linear and therefore well adapted to standard statistical technique. In any case it can be regarded as a first-order approximation to the 'true' relation, because by Taylor's theorem (see Glaister 1977, chapter 16)

$$f(p) = f(p_0) + \frac{df(p_0)}{dp}(p - p_0) + \tfrac{1}{2}\frac{d^2 f(p_0)}{dp^2}(p - p_0)^2 + \dots$$

where p_0 is some 'typical' price level (say, the average in the data). Then, ignoring the quadratic and higher-order terms, we have

$$f(p) - f(p_0) \simeq \frac{df(p_0)}{dp}(p - p_0)$$

or

$$\frac{f(p) - f(p_0)}{f(p_0)} \sim \frac{p_0}{f(p_0)} \frac{df(p_0)}{dp} \frac{p - p_0}{p_0}$$

$$= \eta \frac{p - p_0}{p_0} \qquad (3.6)$$

This states that the proportionate change in demand for a unit proportionate change in price may be approximated by the point elasticity, so long as the price change is sufficiently small for the neglect of the higher-order terms in the Taylor expansion to be acceptable.

3.2 Costs

The *cost function, $c(y)$* say, is *a function relating the level of output y to the total cost of providing it.* It is important to note that unless qualified 'cost' refers to the *minimum possible* cost of producing the specified output level. It is implicit then that in determining cost the supplier will have carried out an optimization, choosing the cheapest set of input levels given their prices which will allow the output to be produced. This is precisely analogous to the consumer's determination of the expenditure function described in section 2.5.

Thus the chosen combination of inputs, as well as the over-all minimum cost, will depend upon the prices of all goods used as inputs (in particular labour). If a supplier could produce his outputs using less of any one of his inputs, or could produce more output from his current inputs then he would not be minimizing his costs. Such a producer is said to be *technically inefficient.* Efficiency is necessary but not sufficient for cost minimization.

Economic inefficiency is precluded by assumption in the definition of the cost function. Although it is extremely important — possibly the most important single factor from the point of view of public policy (see, for example, Foster 1971) — its sources are diverse and institutional and it is therefore difficult to develop a general theory about it.

To press the analogy with consumer behaviour as expressed in (2.28), the producer's cost minimization problem, if he is producing good 1, and assuming that the prices of all goods are constant to him, will be to

$$\text{minimize} \sum_{i=2}^{n} w_i y_i + F \text{ subject to a given value for } y_1$$

$$(3.7)$$

where F is the level of fixed cost per unit time: that is, the level of cost which is invariant to the choice of any of the input or output levels and which must be incurred if the producer is to operate at all. The w_i are input prices.

We may replace the $g(\mathbf{p}, \bar{u})$ of (2.31) with the producer's cost function, $c(\mathbf{w}, y_1)$, the latter being abbreviated $c(y_1)$ as above. The cost function has all the properties enjoyed by the expenditure function. In particular, just as the latter is the dual to the utility function, so the cost function is dual to the *production function*:

$$y_1 = F(y_2, y_3, \ldots, y_n) \qquad (3.8)$$

which expresses *the maximum output that can be attained from the specified input levels*. The quantity

$$F_i(y_2, \ldots, y_n) = \frac{\partial F(y_2, \ldots, y_n)}{\partial y_i}$$

is the rate at which output increases as input of good i is increased and it is known as the *marginal product* of input i. The marginal product of labour, $\partial F/\partial y_n$, is a particularly important example. The assumption of strict quasi-concavity of this function, necessary to achieve the duality referred to above, implies that these *marginal products must be diminishing*, i.e.

$$\partial^2 F/\partial y_i^2 < 0$$

Further it is often assumed that $F(y_2, \ldots, y_n)$ is *strictly* concave which in turn implies that

$$kF(y_2, \ldots, y_n) > F(ky_2, \ldots, ky_n) \quad \text{for} \quad k > 1$$

$$(3.9)$$

The latter statement says that *an equiproportionate increase in all input levels will enable a less than proportionate increase in output*. This is known as the assumption of *decreasing returns to scale*. An equality in (3.9) for all values of k defines constant returns to scale and a reverse inequality with $k > 1$ defines increasing returns to scale. In the latter case two small firms will require more inputs (and hence incur higher costs in total) to produce a given aggregate output than will one large firm. There will therefore be a natural tendency for the industry to consist of a few large firms (*oligopoly*) or just one firm (*monopoly*). The question of whether particular industries in fact display increasing or decreasing technological returns to scale is therefore central to the discussion in chapter 9 of regulation and policy towards competition.

The Lagrangian for (3.7) is given by

$$L(y, \lambda) = \sum_{i=2}^{n} w_i y_i + \lambda [y_1 - F(y_2, \ldots, y_n)] \quad (3.10)$$

where y_1 is the fixed level of output. The necessary conditions for the minimization are therefore

$$w_i = \lambda \frac{\partial F}{\partial y_i} \quad i = 2, \ldots, n \quad (3.11)$$

or

$$\frac{w_j}{w_i} = \frac{\partial F/\partial y_j}{\partial F/\partial y_i} \quad (3.12)$$

This may be compared with (2.5), and states that the ratio of the marginal products must equal the ratio of input prices. By analogy with (2.8) the right of (3.12) is also the rate at which input i must be substituted for j in order to maintain constant output; it is also known as the *marginal rate of substitution* of good i for j. Strict quasi-concavity of the production function is sufficient to guarantee that the solutions to (3.11) yield a cost minimum. The value of the latter at constant prices is, as stated above, denoted by $c(y_1)$.

The maximization of profit requires the choice of an output level which achieves a balance between revenue $R(y_1)$ and minimum cost. Profit is given by

$$\pi(y_1) = R(y_1) - c(y_1) \qquad (3.13)$$

The necessary condition for the maximization of this is then that

$$\frac{dR(y_1)}{dy_1} = \frac{dc(y_1)}{dy_1} \qquad (3.14)$$

This fundamental relationship simply states that at a maximum of profit it must be the case that *marginal revenue be equal to marginal cost*; that is, that the revenue from selling an extra unit just matches the cost of producing it.

Using (3.5) to rewrite (3.14) in terms of the demand elasticity for good 1 faced by the individual operator, we have

$$p_1 \left(1 + \frac{1}{\eta_1}\right) = \frac{dc(y_1)}{dy_1} \qquad (3.15)$$

It is natural to assume that marginal cost is non-negative because it costs more to produce more. Hence it must be that $\eta_1 < -1$ and it also follows that the price charged in equilibrium will be above marginal cost.

The sufficiency condition which guarantees that (3.14) yields a maximum is

$$\frac{d^2R(y_1)}{dy_1^2} - \frac{d^2c(y_1)}{dy_1^2} < 0 \qquad (3.16)$$

In other words marginal cost must be increasing faster than marginal revenue.

3.3 The long run and short run

The account of cost minimization we have just given is, as a matter of definition, said to be a *long run* analysis because it was implicitly assumed that the *quantities of all inputs could be varied* at will. However, labour cannot often be hired and fired instantaneously and variation in the size of a vehicle fleet or the infrastructure may take a considerable time to effect. Short run considerations — those during which *at least one factor of production cannot be varied* — are therefore important.

Because long run cost is the minimum cost of producing a given output when there is freedom to vary all inputs, short run cost cannot be less than long run. For the same reason the long run *marginal* cost of securing an increase in output must be less than the short run marginal cost, and the long run marginal saving of securing a reduction in output must be greater than in the short run.

One possibility we have not mentioned is that at maximum profit revenues do not cover costs. If this is so in the long run then the enterprise cannot operate without some form of subsidy. Profits are maximized — or rather losses are minimized — by ceasing to trade. In the short run, by definition, there will be some fixed costs which are avoidable in the long run. The short run decision about whether an enterprise, or a particular activity within an enterprise, should operate in order to maximize profit then hinges on whether the revenue would cover the variable cost. The fixed cost is unavoidable in any event and so a service may as well be operated if it can cover the variable costs incurred on its behalf and make a contribution to the remaining costs. The question of whether an overall profit is made is largely irrelevant in the short run. A similar situation often exists in the long run with respect to particular services within a group of services. This may be so if there are overhead costs or joint costs which cannot be reduced by withdrawing the service under consideration. Foster (1971) has a useful discussion of the practical problems of defining and measuring costs and he offers some solutions. The arbitrary allocation of such costs to services may be a convenient accounting device, but it is irrelevant and can be very misleading in taking decisions on whether to offer services so as to increase overall net revenues. For example, a certain airline found that despite careful scheduling it had an aircraft standing idle for two hours every day between flights. It was proposed that it should operate a return flight to a nearby destination within the two hours. Although a good load factor could not have been expected it was fairly certain that the flight would generate sufficient revenue to cover the additional costs it would incur. However, the proposal was rejected because those who took the decision costed the flight at a cost per aircraft mile obtained by dividing the total annual airline costs by total annual aircraft mileage. These costs contain a substantial component not attributable to the flight in question and the result was that the proposal was apparently to make a 'loss'.

The extent to which costs do vary in the long run as particular services are varied is both of fundamental importance and difficult to determine in practice. The railways have traditionally maintained that once track and signalling are provided and maintained at a standard sufficient to carry passenger services then costs are largely invariant to the frequency and speed of services which are operated. Joy (1973) caused controversy by questioning whether this is in fact the case in the long run.

The problem in (3.7) is a special case of what is known as a non-linear programming problem. In its general form it may be written as

$$\text{maximize} \quad f(\mathbf{x})$$

$$\text{subject to} \quad g_1(\mathbf{x}) \geqslant 0, g_2(\mathbf{x}) \geqslant 0, \dots, g_m(\mathbf{x}) \geqslant 0$$

where $\mathbf{x} = (x_1, x_2, \dots, x_n)$ is a vector of variables and each of the inequalities expresses a constraint which values of $\mathbf{x}$ must satisfy. A common example in economics is the condition that $x_i \geqslant 0$, when negative-valued quantities are infeasible. A minimization problem may be accommodated by writing $-f(\mathbf{x})$ for the objective, and an equality constraint, such as appears in (3.7), can be expressed as the two inequalities,

$$g_1(x) \geqslant 0 \quad \text{and} \quad -g_1(x) \geqslant 0$$

There are powerful theorems concerning the general properties of non-linear programming problems and a large literature on methods of solution; Intrilligator (1971) and Glaister (1978) give discussions of these. We have assumed in this book that the functions used are non-linear and that the problems can be solved by means of the differential calculus. The special case where the objective and all the constraints are linear functions is known as a *linear programme* and it cannot be solved in this way. It has found important applications in the field of transport.

One class of such problems is known as the 'transportatio-problem', an example of which would be to find the cheapest way of distributing goods to retailers from wholesale depots when limited stocks are available, where the costs of sending items from a given depot to a given retailer are directly proportional to the number of items sent.

There are two particular features of linear programmes which makes them useful in certain circumstances. One is the extreme flexibility with which the constraints that one tends to meet in practical problems can be incorporated, provided that they can be approximated by linear forms. The other is that solution techniques have been developed which guarantee (at considerable increase in computation cost) that the solution values of the choice variables will be whole numbers. This is obviously an advantage in applications where indivisibilities are significant relative to the scale of the problem: aircraft or shipping investments for a small operator, for instance. Excellent texts by Dorfman, Samuelson and Solow (1958) and Gale (1960) discuss the economics of and methods of solution for linear models. Layard and Walters (1978) give a useful discussion of the relationship between them and the 'neoclassical' models used in this book. Chisholm and O'Sullivan (1973) discuss an application to freight flows in the British economy.

3.4 Perfect competition

In general, the more competitors a firm faces in selling its product, the more sensitive will be the demand for its own output to variations in the price it charges. If the number of competitors increases indefinitely each firm will find itself becoming an insignificant contributor to the market. A market price will then rule and any individual firm will have to accept it and behave as a *price taker*. This limiting state is known as *perfect competition*, and is represented in (3.15) by taking the limit as $\eta_1 \to -\infty$. Thus we obtain the result that the marginal revenue for a price taking firm is constant and equal to the selling price, which must in turn equal marginal cost for a profit maximum. The sufficiency condition (3.16) simply requires that marginal cost be increasing, which will clearly be the case if the production function exhibits decreasing returns to scale.

If returns to scale, and hence marginal cost, should be constant, as is frequently assumed, the given price can only equal marginal cost in special circumstances. If this happens then all output levels yield the same profit level, which is zero apart from any element of fixed cost. If the given price does not happen to equal the constant marginal cost a price taking, profit maximizing firm cannot be in equilibrium because it can always improve its position by either indefinitely increasing or decreasing its output to zero. Thus if a competitive industry with constant returns to scale is to be in equilibrium the price must be determined by the marginal cost and the industry size must adjust to the demand forthcoming at that price. This is sometimes known as the *supply price*. The features of such an industry are therefore that the price is determined by supply conditions, independently of demand and the size of any one firm and the number of firms is indeterminate. One would therefore expect to find a wide range of firm sizes. The report of the Committee of Inquiry into Operator's Licensing (1979) seems to indicate that some sectors of the UK road haulage industry have this structure. An example of an industry which would probably have this structure were it not for the regulation of fares is the London taxicab trade (see Beesley 1979). The same is probably true of the bus industry, although there is some doubt about the extent of 'network' economies (see Walters 1979).

It should be noted that when the demand elasticity facing a firm is not infinite the equilibrium price will be above marginal cost, whereas a perfectly competitive firm will set price equal to marginal cost. In the former case the firm is said to enjoy a degree of *monopoly power*. As we shall see in the following chapter this observation forms the basis of some of the classical objections to the 'exploitation' by firms of monopolistic positions.

It is a simple matter to demonstrate that if returns to scale are decreasing, so that marginal costs are increasing, then marginal costs may be above average costs per unit. If so a price taker will be able to earn a profit on his output – or at least, a contribution towards fixed cost. The traditional model of competition would then argue that, if there are no barriers to the entry of new firms to the industry, such firms will eventually enter and drive the price down to the point of zero profit — although a particularly efficient firm with lower costs than most might maintain some residual profit. Conversely, selling price would be below average costs in an 'overpopulated' industry and the least efficient firms would eventually be driven out to the point where industry profits were again close to zero. In practice there are many reasons why this may not happen — there are many ways in which an element of monopoly power may be established and maintained. Particularly important ones in the transport field are collusion to form cartels or conferences and the existence of regulation and licensing.

In the fully competitive situation only the most efficient firms would be able to survive because any firm incurring costs which others do not incur, or missing revenues which the others catch will find itself making a loss. This is the automatic discipline and spur to economic efficiency which the perfectly competitive market provides. We return to this discussion in the next chapter on welfare economics and in chapter 9 on licensing and regulation.

3.5 The supply function

Whether the industry is competitive or not one can postulate selling price as a parameter to the individual firm and calculate *the number of units it would like to produce and sell at each price level*. The resulting relationship between price and output is known as the *supply function* for the firm. By aggregation across firms the industry supply function may be derived. The supply function is the exact counterpart of the market demand function derived in the previous chapter and the joint analysis of demand and supply is discussed in section 3.7.

3.6 Monopolistic behaviour

Because so many of the transport industries are monopolistic or oligopolistic it is worthwhile presenting a little more analysis of monopolistic behaviour. We have seen that for a profit maximizer the fundamental decision rule is that marginal revenue should equal marginal cost. To reiterate (3.15),

$$p_1 \left(1 + \frac{1}{\eta_1}\right) = \frac{dc(y_1)}{dy_1}$$

As we have seen, since marginal cost is positive this must imply an equilibrium with an absolute elasticity greater than unity and also price being higher than marginal cost. Since a competitive industry would be expected to price at marginal cost we may conclude that the effect of monopoly is to sell fewer units at a higher price. The monopoly is said to restrict output.

Suppose now that the monopoly sells two distinct services at prices p_1 and p_2, and the demands are given by $y_1 = f_1(p_1, p_2)$ and $y_2 = f_2(p_1, p_2)$. Then the overall profit is given by

$$\pi = p_1 y_1 - c_1(y_1) + p_2 y_2 - c_2(y_2)$$
$$= p_1 f_1(p_1, p_2) - c_1[f_1(p_1, p_2)] + p_2 f_2(p_1, p_2)$$
$$- c_2[f_2(p_1, p_2)] \quad (3.17)$$

Then for a profit maximum the two prices must be set so that

$$p_1 \left(1 + \frac{1}{\eta_{11}}\right) = \frac{dc_1(y_1)}{dy_1} - \left(p_2 - \frac{dc_2(y_2)}{dy_2}\right) \frac{y_2}{y_1} \frac{\eta_{21}}{\eta_{11}}$$
$$(3.18)$$
$$p_2 \left(1 + \frac{1}{\eta_{22}}\right) = \frac{dc_2(y_2)}{dy_1} - \left(p_1 - \frac{dc_1(y_1)}{dy_1}\right) \frac{y_1}{y_2} \frac{\eta_{12}}{\eta_{22}}$$

where here η_{11} and η_{22} are the two normal own-price elasticities and η_{ij} are the cross-price elasticities of demand for service i with respect to a change in price of service j. If the demands for the two services were entirely independent then the cross-price elasticities would be zero, but if the increase of one price is expected to cause some users to switch to the other service (i.e. they are substitutes) then they will be positive. In order to interpret (3.18) suppose first that the markets are independent of each other and suppose that the marginal costs of providing the services are the same. Suppose however, that the elasticity in market one is much lower than that in market two. Then (3.18) indicates that the price in market one will be higher in the less elastic market, despite the fact that the costs of provision are the same. This is known as *price discrimination* or 'charging what the market will bear'. A good and common example is the provision of first and second class travel. Here the costs of supplying a seat mile are very similar but two different travelling groups can be identified having differing demand characteristics. Very often these are business and leisure markets but other identifiable groups are the old and students, both of which are sometimes offered special rates. Another example was in the fixing of railway freight rates in the nineteenth century where the fact that the transport costs comprised a relatively small proportion of the total costs of high value goods meant that they tended to exhibit relatively low elasticities with respect to the rate charged. Price discrimination led to relatively high rates on high value goods and low rates on low value bulk goods despite the fact that the latter generally cost more to carry.

In practice there are complications. It is often difficult to entirely separate the markets so that, for instance, some business travellers will choose to take second class seats as the price differential between the two classes widens. In other words the cross-price elasticities are not zero but positive. Since prices in both markets will exceed their marginal costs the terms in parentheses on the right-hand sides in (3.18) will both be positive. Since both own-price elasticities are negative it follows that the possibility of switching between markets makes both prices further above their respective marginal costs than they otherwise would be. This is to be expected because raising the price in one market generates more revenue in the other.

Referring again to (3.18), suppose now that the demand elasticities are rather similar but that there is a wide divergence of marginal costs. A good example here, which is discussed at greater length in chapter 5, is the distinction between a market served in the peak (say market one) and one served in the off-peak. Then because supplying a marginal unit in the peak involves the provision of extra capacity, peak marginal costs will generally be substantially higher than off-peak marginal costs, and so one would expect a profit maximizing operator to adopt higher prices in the peak. The cross-price terms in (3.18) indicate that the possibilities of directing some of the demand from the peak to the off-peak are also relevant here.

In practice one would expect the profit maximizing monopolist to exhibit elements of both price discrimination and peak pricing. Note that one would also expect a competitive trade to vary its prices because of increases in marginal costs at peaks, but it would *not* adopt price discrimination because competitive prices will always be determined by costs. As we show in chapter 4, although variation in line with differing costs is justified in the interests of economic efficiency, this has occasionally not been recognized in regulatory legislation, with the result that carriers have been forced to take at unduly low rates as much bulky, low value and expensive-to-carry goods as have been presented, whilst being forced to discourage light, high value goods by charging high rates although they would have been cheap to carry. This can introduce an element of cross-subsidization which is undesirable from the point of view of the overall 'public interest'. That would require that each user should face the true marginal cost that he causes by his actions.

The analysis in this chapter has been in terms of the ideal of cost minimization and technical efficiency. In practice this can never be fully achieved for reasons ranging from the difficulties of transmitting information in large organizations, inferior management and confusion about objectives to restrictive practices enforced by labour unions and government imposed regulations on conditions at work and employment. Interesting studies of the practical problems in UK public enterprises have been published by Pryke (1971), Pryke and Dodgeson (1975), Foster (1971) and Gwilliam *et al.* (1980).

3.7 Market equilibrium and comparative statics

In chapter 2 we derived the total demand function for a good, denoted, say, by

$$x = f(p) \quad \text{with} \quad f'(p) < 0$$

and in this chapter we have derived the total industry supply function denoted, say, by

$$y = g(p) \quad \text{with} \quad g'(p) > 0$$

The former states the number of units consumers would like to buy at each price and the latter states the number of units that the industry would like to sell at each price. An *equilibrium price* is any solution to the equation

$$f(p) = g(p) \tag{3.19}$$

that is, a price at which the number of units consumers wish to buy is consistent with the number producers would like to sell. Such a solution may not exist (for instance if the maximum price that consumers are willing to pay falls short of the minimum price that producers require for their first unit). We shall assume that a solution does exist at a strictly positive price, and further that it is unique. Call the equilibrium price p^*. Then if at some point in time $p > p^*$ there will be an excess supply of the good and its price will tend to fall. Conversely if $p < p^*$ there will be an excess demand for the good and its price will tend to rise. This is consistent with the assumption that the market for the good is *globally stable*, that is that given any initial price level it will adjust, given sufficient time, until equilibrium is reached. This is not a trivial assumption as it is quite easy to construct simple and realistic models of adjustment which are not stable (see, for example, Glaister 1978).

However, assuming that there exists a unique and stable equilibrium we now wish to illustrate a method of analysing the response of the equilibrium to various changes in circumstances. For instance, suppose that demand increases exogenously. Then introducing a *shift parameter* α to represent the increased demand, the equilibrium is defined by

$$f(p) + \alpha = g(p) \tag{3.20}$$

This defines the solution price as an implicit function of α.

Differentiating (3.12) with respect to α yields

$$\frac{\mathrm{d}f(p)}{\mathrm{d}p} \frac{\mathrm{d}p}{\mathrm{d}x} + 1 = \frac{\mathrm{d}g(p)}{\mathrm{d}p} \frac{\mathrm{d}p}{\mathrm{d}\alpha}$$

Hence

$$\frac{\mathrm{d}p}{\mathrm{d}\alpha} = \frac{1}{g'(p) - f'(p)} \qquad (3.21)$$

This is a positive number, showing that the price will rise in a free market. The price rise has the double effect of mitigating the increase in demand and causing an increase in supply, so that a new equilibrium can be established. Formula (3.21) might, for example, be used to predict the effect of increased demand for road haulage or oil tanker services on freight rates in terms of the slopes of the demand and supply relations.

As a second example, suppose that a tax is imposed of 100% paid by the producer so that the supply function becomes

$$x = g(p - t) \qquad (3.22)$$

Now let p be price net of tax; then we have the implicit relations in p:

$$f[p(t)] = g[\hat{p}(t)] \qquad \hat{p}(t) = p(t) - t$$

Differentiating by the chain rule:

$$\frac{\mathrm{d}f(p)}{\mathrm{d}p} \frac{\mathrm{d}p}{\mathrm{d}t} = \frac{\mathrm{d}g(\hat{p})}{\mathrm{d}\hat{p}} \frac{\mathrm{d}\hat{p}}{\mathrm{d}t}$$

$$= \frac{\mathrm{d}g(\hat{p})}{\mathrm{d}\hat{p}} \left(\frac{\mathrm{d}p}{\mathrm{d}t} - 1\right)$$

Hence

$$\frac{\mathrm{d}p}{\mathrm{d}t} = \frac{-\mathrm{d}g/\mathrm{d}\hat{p}}{\mathrm{d}f/\mathrm{d}p - \mathrm{d}g/\mathrm{d}\hat{p}}$$

Now, assuming simply that $\mathrm{d}f/\mathrm{d}p < 0$ and $\mathrm{d}g/\mathrm{d}\hat{p} > 0$, we immediately have that

$$0 < \mathrm{d}p/\mathrm{d}t < 1$$

so that 'the price goes up, but by an amount less than the

tax'. Further,

$$\frac{dp}{dt} = \frac{-(1/g)\,(dg/d\hat{p})}{(1/g)\,(df/dp) - (1/g)\,(dg/d\hat{p})}$$

$$= \frac{-(1/g)\,(dg/d\hat{p})}{(1/f)\,(df/dp) - (1/g)\,(dg/d\hat{p})}$$

since $f(p) = g(p)$. But

$$\frac{p}{f}\frac{df(p)}{dp} = \epsilon, \quad \frac{\hat{p}}{g}\frac{dg}{d\hat{p}} = \mu$$

say, where ϵ and μ are the elasticities of demand and supply, respectively. So

$$\frac{dp}{dt} = \frac{\mu/\hat{p}}{\mu/\hat{p} - \epsilon/p}$$

This tells us a great deal; for instance, if $\epsilon = 0$, $dp/dt = 1$; in other words, if the demand is completely inelastic, the whole tax is passed on. Similarly

$$\lim_{\mu \to \infty} \frac{dp}{dt} = 1 \quad \lim_{\mu \to 0} \frac{dp}{dt} = 0$$

$$\lim_{t \to 0} \frac{dp}{dt} = \frac{\mu}{\mu - \epsilon}$$

a rather neat result. The reader should be able to interpret these results easily by a graphical analysis.

What of tax revenue? This is given by

$$R = tf[p(t)]$$

so

$$\frac{dR}{dt} = f(p) + t\frac{df(p)}{dp}\frac{dp}{dt}$$

$$= f(p)\left(1 - \frac{t\epsilon}{p}\frac{\mu/\hat{p}}{\epsilon/\hat{p} - \mu/p}\right)$$

In particular, if $\mu \to \infty$, it will be possible to both reduce consumption and simultaneously raise revenue if

$$1 + t\epsilon/p > 0 \quad \text{or} \quad t\epsilon/p > -1$$

Revenue will be maximized if

$$t\epsilon/p = -1$$

Notice particularly that these results do depend on the assumption that the new equilibrium is in fact attained. If the market was unstable equilibrium would never be attained; even if stable it might take a 'long time' for the market to get close to an equilibrium. The actual dynamic path of adjustment is not considered. Since we are comparing one long-term equilibrium with another, the method is called *comparative statics*.

The likely impact of a change in taxation on the number of units bought and sold, and on tax revenue is an important issue in transport. For instance, how will changes in fuel tax, licence fees and vehicle excise duties affect the ownership and use of vehicles? How will an increased landing fee at an airport affect the number of air passengers? By how much will tax rates on heavy vehicles have to be raised or lowered to make them cover the maintenance costs they impose on roads? The comparative static analysis illustrates that the answers to these questions will depend critically upon the relationships between the demand and supply elasticities.

4 Welfare Economics

The phrases *economically efficient allocation of resources* and *Pareto optimum* mean the same thing. In an economy primary resources are allocated to firms. They combine them to make the goods and services which are eventually allocated to final consumers. Some of the primary resources like labour are provided by the consumers themselves. An allocation of commodities is said to be economically efficient if *it cannot be changed in such a way as to make any one consumer or producer better off unless somebody else is simultaneously made worse off*. The proposition that an economically inefficient allocation is something that one should seek to eliminate seems to be commonly accepted and is central to this book.

The purpose of this chapter is to sketch a series of propositions which lead to the 'fundamental theorem of welfare economics'. Roughly this says that on certain assumptions, if the prices of all goods and services (including labour) are determined in perfectly competitive markets then the allocation which results from individuals maximizing their utilities (as in chapter 2) and firms maximizing their profits (as in chapter 3) at these prices will be economically efficient:

A competitive equilibrium is a Pareto optimum

There is a converse. In general an economy will have infinitely many Pareto optima. Different ones will have different distributions of welfare amongst individuals and which one emerges will depend upon the tax system and the distribution of basic endowments amongst individuals, such as ownership of resources, possession of skills and abilities amongst indi-

viduals. The converse states that if any arbitrary Pareto
optimum is selected then *it may be achieved through the
competitive price system providing that an appropriate set of
taxes and initial endowments is selected*.

If one is seeking guidance on the 'correct' price for a particular commodity and if it can be assumed that all other
commodities on which this price has any bearing are traded
in competitive markets, then the theorem indicates that in
order to achieve a Pareto optimum it is necessary that a competitive market be 'aped' for the commodity in question. In
other words the price should be set at marginal production
cost (see section 3.4). If there are non-competitive features
in the other markets then things are more complicated but in
some cases the 'theory of the second best' provides guidance
as to how the simple marginal cost rules should be modified,
and this is illustrated in chapter 5.

The following is a much simplified and shortened account.
Layard and Walters (1978) give a longer one. Debreu (1959)
gives the definitive treatment using powerful topological
techniques as does Malinvaud (1972) in his text.

4.1 The conditions necessary for economic efficiency

To simplify the exposition we assume that there are two
individuals who derive utility from the consumption of two
goods x and y according to $U(x_u, y_u)$ and $V(x_v, y_v)$. The
goods are produced by two firms which consume primary
resources A and B as inputs according to the production
functions $X(A_x, B_x)$ and $Y(A_y, B_y)$. The conditions

$$x_u + x_v = X(A_x, B_x) \qquad (\mu_x)$$
$$y_u + y_v = Y(A_y, B_y) \qquad (\mu_y)$$

$$(4.1)$$

state that total demand should equal total supply for the two
final products. The conditions

$$A_x + A_y = A \qquad (\gamma_A)$$
$$B_x + B_y = B \qquad (\gamma_B)$$

$$(4.2)$$

state the same thing for the primary resources. The problem

is, given total primary resources A and B to allocate them between the two firms, and to allocate the output of the two firms between the two individuals so as to achieve an economically efficient allocation. The latter may be characterized by varying the allocation so as to maximize the utility attained by one individual whilst holding that attained by the other constant. Maximizing $U(\cdot)$, using the Lagrangian multipliers as indicated with the feasibility constraints in (4.1) and (4.2) and the multiplier λ for the constraint which specifies that $V(\cdot)$ be held constant gives the following conditions:

$$\frac{\partial U}{\partial x_u} = \mu_x \qquad \frac{\partial U}{\partial y_u} = \mu_y \qquad (4.3)$$

$$\lambda \frac{\partial V}{\partial x_v} = \mu_x \qquad \lambda \frac{\partial V}{\partial \dot{y}_v} = \mu_y \qquad (4.4)$$

$$\mu_x \frac{\partial X}{\partial A_x} = \gamma_A \qquad \mu_x \frac{\partial X}{\partial B_x} = \gamma_B \qquad (4.5)$$

$$\mu_y \frac{\partial Y}{\partial A_y} = \gamma_A \qquad \mu_y \frac{\partial Y}{\partial B_v} = \gamma_B \qquad (4.6)$$

These somewhat complicated conditions have straightforward interpretations. From (4.3) and (4.4)

$$\frac{\partial U/\partial x_u}{\partial U/\partial y_u} = \frac{\mu_x}{\mu_y} = \frac{\partial V/\partial x_v}{\partial V/\partial y_v} \qquad (4.7)$$

Conditions (4.7) imply that the marginal rates of substitution between the two goods should be the same for the two individuals and should be equal to a common ratio of shadow prices. This is known as efficiency in exchange. If it were not satisfied the two individuals could negotiate a rate of exchange of one good against the other (that is a *relative price*) so that by trading with each other on these terms they would *both* be better off. The benefits of such a process are sometimes known as 'gains from trade'.

Analogously, (4.5) and (4.6) give

$$\frac{\partial X/\partial A_x}{\partial X/\partial B_x} = \frac{\gamma_A}{\gamma_B} = \frac{\partial Y/\partial A_y}{\partial Y/\partial B_y} \qquad (4.8)$$

These conditions for the firms parallel (4.7) and if they were not satisfied the firms could arrange mutual exchange so that more of both outputs could be produced from the same total resources. Another deduction from (4.5) and (4.6) is

$$\frac{\partial Y/\partial A_y}{\partial X/\partial A_x} = \frac{\mu_x}{\mu_y} = \frac{\partial Y/\partial B_y}{\partial X/\partial B_x} \tag{4.9}$$

The left-hand side of (4.9) is the sacrifice of output of y that would be necessary if one more unit of x were to be produced by transferring resource A from one firm to the other. This is known as the marginal rate of transformation of y into x. It must be the same at the margin if resource B is transferred rather than A. The common ratio in (4.9) is the same as in (4.7) so that the marginal rate of transformation must equal the marginal rates of substitution for both consumers.

We can now make the main point of this chapter. Suppose that prices p_x and p_y are established for the goods and that both consumers, believing themselves to comprise an insignificant proportion of the demand, maximize their utilities taking the prices as given. Then condition (2.5) shows that they will both set their marginal rates of substitution equal to the price ratio. Hence (4.7), one of the necessary conditions for a Pareto optimum, will be met.

Suppose now that the primary resources A and B are bought by the firms in competition at prices w_A and w_B. The firms believe themselves to be insignificant parts of the economy and so maximize their profits taking the ruling input and output prices as given: for example maximize

$$p_x X (A_x, B_x) - w_A A_x - w_B B_x$$

This gives the first-order conditions for firm x:

$$p_x \frac{\partial X}{\partial A_x} = w_A \qquad p_x \frac{\partial X}{\partial B_x} = w_B \tag{4.10}$$

and for firm y:

$$p_y \frac{\partial Y}{\partial A_y} = w_A \qquad p_y \frac{\partial Y}{\partial B_y} = w_B \tag{4.11}$$

Conditions (4.10) and (4.11) are directly comparable with

(4.5) and (4.6) showing that the remaining necessary conditions for Pareto optimality, (4.8) and (4.9), will be satisfied. These conditions will be sufficient if the utility functions are strictly quasi-concave and there are no increasing returns in production.

4.2 The fundamental theorem

We have now illustrated the fundamental proposition outlined at the beginning of the chapter: if an equilibrium is established by entirely free competition then the price system which is established will have the property that agents acting in their own interests will collectively lead to an economically efficient allocation of resources. Note particularly that, as we observed in chapter 3, conditions like (4.10) for profit maximization by a competitive firm amount to a statement that *price should equal marginal cost.*

These results obviously apply to an idealized economy. They are useful in providing a standard against which a real problem can be evaluated. In some cases it is arguable that the reality is sufficiently close to the ideal for the results to be of direct application. In other cases it is instructive to analyse the respects in which the reality renders the ideal inapplicable. We therefore now mention some of the more important assumptions that are necessary.

Perhaps the most fundamental are embraced in the phrase 'perfect competition'. This requires that every agent is a price taker. There must be no element of monopoly amongst sellers or monopoly amongst buyers. This rules out the activities of cartels, labour unions and so on. Every agent has full knowledge of the prices and characteristics of all goods available now and in the future. There is no uncertainty about future states of the world. If any of these assumptions is not satisfied then there is 'market failure' and this simplistic theory will require a suitable modification to deal with the particular problem at hand, or possibly complete rejection. Layard and Walters (1978) detail some of the ways in which market failures can be dealt with.

A second group of assumptions concerns the independence of agents from each other. The level of consumption of one individual does not affect directly the utility of any other. Traffic congestion (see chapter 5) is an example of an *externality* where this assumption does not hold. Similarly the activities of firms do not affect consumers; for example there is no pollution. Firms neither help nor hinder each other — there are no external economies or diseconomies. Apple growing and bee keeping are the classic examples of two activities having beneficial externalities.

It will be noted that the common marginal rates of substitution in (2.5) are equal to the ratios of the market prices faced by consumers. In the case of (4.7) they are equal to the ratios of the shadow prices on the constraints in (4.1). Now, a shadow price measures the increase in the objective that could be achieved if the respective constraint were relaxed by one unit. In this case μ_x is the extra utility available to $U(\cdot)$, whilst holding $V(\cdot)$ constant, if one more unit of x were to become available; similarly for μ_y. The ratio is therefore the net rate of change of social benefit if units of y are exchanged for units of x. In other words it is the social opportunity cost of a unit of x in terms of units of y. It follows that in a competitive equilibrium the relative prices of commodities are equal to their relative social values.

This is a most important result from the point of view of the practical cost benefit analysis of a transport infrastructure investment because it means that if it can be assumed that all the relevant markets are in full competitive equilibrium, and there is no 'market failure', then the market prices of the resources used by a project can be taken to represent their social values. If, on the other hand, there is some form of market failure it may be necessary to modify or replace market prices by shadow prices which more accurately reflect true social opportunity costs (see for example, McKean 1968, for a detailed discussion). A commonly quoted example of this is labour in an economy where the labour market is not in equilibrium and there is unemployment. Then the cost of using unemployed labour may be very low because it does not have to be removed from an alternative productive use, and the wage rate would therefore be a serious overestimate.

Assuming market failures not to occur we see that the

market price, which represents the private cost of consumption to the consumer, is the marginal private cost of production to the firm and the marginal social cost. The fundamental theorem implies that for Pareto optimality it is necessary that marginal private cost should equal marginal social cost for all goods and for all agents. This result crops up in several guises in the next chapter.

A purist might argue that an economist should only advocate a proposal which he could demonstrate to be a Pareto improvement, because only then could he be sure that nobody would lose by the move. There would probably be no dispute about the ethics of making some people better off at no one else's expense. In practice almost any proposal involves both gainers and losers and the strict requirement that a Pareto improvement be actually achieved would be so severe as to render economic advice sterile. A much weaker requirement, which does have practical uses, is that a move should produce a *potential* Pareto improvement: that is, *in principle*, the gainers should be able to at least compensate the losers and still remain better off. This has become known as the Hicks–Kaldor criterion. A proposal may be deemed acceptable if it satisfies this criterion even though the lump sum compensations will not in fact be made so that there will be losers at the end of the day.

A test that says that a project is acceptable if the aggregate compensating variation embodied in (2.43) is strictly positive is one that satisfies the Hicks–Kaldor criterion. This is the test we shall implicitly use throughout this book. It implies an agnosticism about the distribution of welfare across individuals, as mentioned in section 2.8.

As an example, imagine once again a bridge in private ownership on which a toll is collected although the marginal cost of allowing a vehicle to cross is negligible (ignore toll collection costs). A proposal is made to legislate to prevent the owner from charging. Since this would achieve a price equal to marginal social cost this proposal would generate a positive aggregate compensating variation as could be demonstrated by arguments similar to those set out in chapter 1. The Hicks–Kaldor criterion would be satisfied: in principle the gainers (users) could pay lump sums unrelated to their use of the bridge so that the losers (owners) would be fully compensated for their lost revenue and there would be a surplus benefit left (in fact equal to an area analogous to D in figure 1.2). In practice it would probably be quite impossible to organize such a system of transfers and there would in fact be losers. The owners might be compensated from the public purse, but in that case the losers would be those tax paying members of the public who derive no benefit from the bridge.

Whilst the Hicks–Kaldor criterion has been found to be a useful one it has been increasingly recognized that it is unreasonable to take decisions on the basis of that alone without taking an explicit view on the position of losers. Lichfield's (1970) 'planning balance sheet' and the similar development for the purpose of planning trunk road investments by the UK Advisory Committee on Trunk Road Assessment (1977 and 1979a) are examples of attempts to rationalize this.

5 Marginal Social Cost Pricing

5.1 Congestion of homogeneous traffic flows

Although the following exposition is much simplified, the point it makes underlies almost all discussions of the economics of congestion. Whilst this phenomenon is important in the study of transport economics it is also common in many other fields, such as telecommunications.

Suppose that all vehicles in a flow of traffic are identical and that there are x such vehicles. Let $c(x)$ be the cost per mile to each vehicle. This is generally assumed to be composed of two main components: money cost and time costs. Both would normally depend upon traffic speed and hence on the level of congestion. The total social cost per mile is given by

$$T(x) = xc(x) \quad \mathrm{d}c(x)/\mathrm{d}x > 0 \tag{5.1}$$

Hence the change in social cost which will occur if one more vehicle joins the flow, that is the *marginal social cost* (MSC), will be given by

$$\mathrm{MSC} = \frac{\mathrm{d}T(x)}{\mathrm{d}x} = c(x) + \frac{\mathrm{d}c(x)}{\mathrm{d}x}$$

$$= c(x)(1 + \eta) \tag{5.2}$$

where

$$\eta = \frac{\mathrm{d}c(x)}{\mathrm{d}x} \frac{x}{c(x)} \tag{5.3}$$

is the elasticity of cost with respect to a change in the number of vehicles. This will normally be strictly positive, a large proportion of the increase being in time costs. We conclude that the cost incurred by the individual vehicle mile will fall short of the total cost that it imposes on society. This is simply because the individual only considers the costs that he incurs himself and does not take account of the fact that his own action will affect all other users. This is a clear example of an externality of the kind mentioned in the previous chapter as a reason for market failure. The argument is developed in some detail by Walters (1961).

Since all individuals are assumed identical the same considerations apply to all. For each one the marginal private cost is less than the marginal social cost. The analysis of chapter 4 would lead one to expect that this would be a source of economic inefficiency. One way of showing this is to use a simple consumer surplus argument to show that it is optimum that the individual should pay a tax (or toll or road price) in order to bring private and social costs together. Let t be a tax per mile for road use. The total private cost per mile may then be given by

$$g = c(x) + t \qquad (5.4)$$

Then if the demand for vehicle mileage is given by

$$x = f(g) \quad \text{with} \quad f'(g) < 0 \qquad (5.5)$$

we may choose the rate of tax so as to maximize the total willingness to pay (see section 2.6) net of resource costs:

$$\int_g^\alpha f(z) \, dz + g f(g) - c(x) f(g) = \int_g^\alpha f(z) \, dz + t f(g) \qquad (5.6)$$

Differentiating with respect to t yields the first-order condition (we assume the relevant second-order condition to be satisfied):

$$-f(g) \frac{dg}{dt} + t \frac{df(g)}{dg} \frac{dg}{dt} + f(g) = 0 \qquad (5.7)$$

But implicit differentiation of (5.4) yields

$$\frac{dg}{dt} = \left(1 - \frac{dc}{dx}\frac{df}{dg}\right)^{-1}$$

and substitution for dg/dt in the first-order condition gives

$$\left(t - \frac{dc}{dx}f(g)\right)\frac{df}{dg} = 0$$

This implies that at the optimum it is necessary that

$$t = f(g)\frac{dc}{dx}$$

Substituting this value of t in the definition of g gives

$$g = c(x) + x\frac{dc}{dx}$$

$$= c(x)(1 + \eta) \tag{5.8}$$

This expression was previously shown to be the marginal social cost, and so we conclude that the optimum tax will be such as to make the private cost equal to the marginal social cost. It will also be the case that the tax with this property will satisfy

$$t/c(x) = \eta$$

or equivalently

$$\frac{t}{g} = \frac{\eta}{1 + \eta} \tag{5.9}$$

which expresses the proportion of private cost constituted by the optimum tax in terms of the private congestion cost elasticity. It should be noted that the optimum tax will in general vary widely at different times of the day and at different places because of the effects of differing conditions and of differing road capacities on this elasticity. It would thus be a mistake to impose a rate of tax which was constant at all times in a city such as London where there are enormous variations in the degree of congestion.

To illustrate, some calculations for London estimate the private generalized cost of a car mile in the central area at £0.26 (at 1979 prices) and the marginal social cost (including costs incurred by commercial vehicles and buses) at £0.363, indicating a cost elasticity of 0.42. But in the inner area the respective figures are £0.23 and £0.466 giving an elasticity of 1.0, and in the outer area they are £0.187 and £0.42 giving an elasticity of 1.25. These figures suggest that a system of optimum taxes would fix very different rates in the different areas of London.

It is important to note the full significance of this result. First, the solution involves a form of marginal cost pricing. Second, by using the consumer surplus method we have evaded the question of the effects of the tax on the income distribution. However, in keeping with the fundamental theorem of welfare economics discussed in the previous chapter, even if the individual users of the facility have different incomes and are affected to different extents by the tax, marginal social cost pricing will be necessary for economic efficiency and there will, in principle, exist a set of lump sum money transfers such that everybody is at least as well off after the tax as before it: the Hicks–Kaldor criterion is satisfied, or, in the language of chapter 2, the sum of all the compensating variations is positive. This is because the existence of an efficient pricing system enables those who value the service most highly to use it and to more than compensate for those who are unable to travel after the imposition of the tax. There is net social gain because the 'deadloss' of resources associated with excessive congestion has been removed. Third, it is important to note that at the optimum there is still a certain amount of congestion: it is *not* optimum to remove the congestion completely. This is typical of optimum congestion rules.

The theory of the welfare distributional effects of road pricing in the absence of lump sum transfers is discussed by Layard (1977). There is a considerable literature on the various technical possibilities for implementing road pricing systems; they are surveyed by Beesley (1973a). A technically simple system was worked out by the Greater London Council (1974). Anyone wishing to use a vehicle in central

London on any particular day between particular times would have to display a licence valid for that day. Subject to certain exceptions and concessions it was proposed that the daily licence fee for cars should be between £0.60 and £1.00 (at 1974 prices) and it was predicted that this would reduce traffic in the central area by about one-third, with net social benefits of £25 million per annum. A tax revenue of £45 million per annum would have been generated which could have been used to alleviate property tax (rates) payments by London residents. In the event this was not implemented. However, a road pricing scheme has more recently been adopted in Singapore and early experience with it has been encouraging (see Watson and Holland 1977).

5.2 Peak load pricing

The problem of the peak load is a severe one and a common one in the transport industries. Examples are urban bus and rail services, airport and airline services, holiday travel facilities and road capacities. Other examples are electricity supply and telecommunications. As an illustration, for accompanied car crossings of the English Channel in 1973 about 1% of the total annual demand occurs during 0.1% of the hours of the year and 40% occurs during the busiest 10% of the year (Glaister 1976). There are several approaches to the problem; some will be found in Williamson (1966) and Rees (1976) and in the references they contain. For simplicity we here make several assumptions, none of which affect the essential economic points of the analysis: the generalization is fairly straightforward.

Let us assume that the demand cycle under consideration occupies one day (very often it will in fact occupy one half day) and that day can be conveniently split into just two parts, the peak and the off-peak, which last respectively for t_1 and t_2 hours. The total numbers of units demanded in the peak and off-peak are given by

$$x_1 = f_1(p_1) \quad \text{and} \quad x_2 = f_2(p_2) \tag{5.10}$$

The costs of providing the units supplied are given by $c_1(x_1)$ and $c_2(x_2)$ excluding any capital costs. The maximum capacity available is K units per hour. Initially we assume that K is variable and that the cost in £ per day of having K units of capacity is given by $r(K)$. The latter would be the daily interest, depreciation and maintenance cost of the capacity. The object is then to choose p_1, p_2 and K according to some suitable criterion. We shall choose net social surplus; it is easy to repeat the following analysis using net profit as an objective. Thus we maximize

$$\int_{p_1}^{\alpha_1} f_1(z)\,dz + p_1 x_1 + \int_{p_2}^{\alpha_2} f_2(z)\,dz + p_2 x_2 - c_1(x_1)$$
$$- c_2(x_2) - r(K) \qquad (5.11)$$

which is willingness to pay, net of resource costs. By regrouping terms this can be interpreted alternatively as consumer's surplus plus profit (the latter is sometimes known as producer's surplus). The maximization must be carried out whilst observing the capacity constraint

$$f_1(p_1) \leqslant Kt_1 \qquad (5.12)$$

We shall implicitly assume that the peak is sufficiently sharp to guarantee that if the capacity constraint is satisfied in the peak then it will also be satisfied in the off-peak.

By introducing a slack variable S, (5.12) can be rewritten as

$$Kt_1 - f_1(p_1) - S = 0 \qquad (5.13)$$

with

$$S \geqslant 0 \qquad (5.14)$$

S is a measure of the degree of excess capacity at the peak.

Using λ as the Lagrangian multiplier for (5.13) with (5.11), gives the first-order conditions

$$-f_1(p_1) + p_1 f_1'(p_1) + f_1(p_1) - c_1' f_1'(p_1) - \lambda f_1'(p_1) = 0$$
$$(5.15)$$

$$-f_2(p_2) + p_2 f_2'(p_2) + f_2(p_2) - c_2' f_2'(p_2) = 0 \qquad (5.16)$$

$$-r'(K) + \lambda t_1 = 0 \qquad (5.17)$$

If $\lambda > 0$ then $S = 0$; $S > 0$ only if $\lambda = 0$ (5.18)

Conditions (5.18) cannot be obtained by differentiating with respect to S, because the Lagrangian is linear in S. It is obtained by elementary reasoning, bearing in mind that the Lagrangian has to be maximized with respect to S.

Considering first (5.17), we have that

$$\lambda = r'(K)/t_1 \qquad (5.19)$$

This simply states that at the optimum the daily cost of obtaining one extra unit of capacity per hour that it will be productive, must equal the extra net social benefit that could be attained from it — the latter being the shadow price on the capacity constraint.

Conditions (5.18) then say that if the marginal cost of capital is positive then capacity must be fully used in the peak; spare capacity can only exist in the peak at the optimum if it is costless to obtain it.

Conditions (5.15) and (5.16) can be rewritten

$$p_1 = c_1' + \frac{1}{t_1} r'(K) \qquad (5.20)$$

$$p_2 = c_2' \qquad (5.21)$$

Condition (5.21) simply states that off-peak price should equal the cost of producing an extra unit. This is a generalization of the familiar classical condition which was stated in one form by Dupuit (1844) when he concluded that in the absence of congestion and with excess capacity, the optimum toll for the use of a bridge is zero if the cost of an extra trip is negligible as it normally will be. This is the basis of the standard case against charging for the use of existing roads when there is spare capacity. On the other hand (5.20) states that the whole of the costs incurred by the purchase of the final unit of capacity should be added to the peak marginal production cost. The division by t_1 is to account for the fact that the capacity costs must be incurred over the whole day whilst the peak only lasts for part of it: the shorter the peak the higher the optimum peak cost. The whole of the marginal capacity costs caused by the peak users should be attributed to them. This is another manifestation of marginal cost pricing; in this case the price to the peak consumer is set equal to the long run cost of providing one extra unit of service. The words 'long run' here indicate that the results apply to the case where the capacity of the enterprise is variable. The short run case where the capacity is fixed is discussed below. The results differ from those that would be attained for a profit maximizing enterprise in that there is no element of price discrimination which would press prices above long run marginal costs in inelastic markets.

There are many examples of transport facilities which suffer severe peak load problems: international airlines, commuter roads and railways, ferries, air and sea ports, bus services and so on. In the UK telecommunications and, to a lesser extent, electricity utilities have illustrated the feasibility and benefits of peak pricing. However, transport operators seem to have been much more cautious in adopting it. It has been evident to a modest degree in some of the more competitive sectors such as holiday air travel, and recently cross-Channel ferries (which face extremely peaked demand conditions) have been persuaded to move in this direction following government pressure and the recommendations of a Monopolies Commission report (1974). On the other hand, almost all bus services charge fares that are uniform by time of day and season of the year with the endorsement of the Traffic Commissioners, and the railways actually adopt the somewhat perverse strategy of offering substantial discounts to season ticket holders who constitute a large portion of the peak traffic on commuting routes.

A common objection to proposals to adopt peak load pricing is that it is 'unfair' to penalize the unfortunate traveller who 'has' to travel in the peak and that price increases in the peak mean that it is the poor who are prevented from travelling. However, as with the congestion pricing argument, to argue this is to miss the point of the analysis. A money price charged for a facility means that in the absence of queues the service is obtained by those who value it most *relative to other things*. If cheap fares are provided at times of severe peaks then the cost to society of building the capacity to cope with these peaks may be very much higher than the values placed on the service even by those who value it most. This is inefficient in the sense of chapter 4 so that long run marginal cost pricing (i.e. peak pricing) together with a suitable system of compensation could make everybody at least as well off as he would be under constant pricing. The 'unfairness' of peak pricing rests on the premise that constant prices are 'fair'. But it is neither fair nor sensible to encourage the poor or anybody else to use a facility which costs society (or travellers at other times) more to provide than the benefits they derive from it. On the other hand, it must be admitted that the imperfect nature of taxation and compensation systems in practice means that inevitably some individuals will in fact be made worse off. This disadvantage has to be set against the welfare losses due to economic inefficiency.

A short run analysis of the problem is appropriate if the level of capacity K cannot be varied. The analysis leading to (5.15), (5.16) and (5.18) is unchanged but (5.17) now has no meaning. Thus (5.20) and (5.21) stand but with λ written for $r'(K)$. The economic prescription is thus similar: off-peak fares should equal marginal operating costs only; peak fares should be increased above peak marginal operating costs by an amount which will just be sufficient to restrict peak demand to the available capacity. It follows as a corollary that, in general, it will be economically inefficient to allow a queue to form at any facility if the alternative of rationing by price together with a compensating redistribution is available.

The distinction between the short and long runs is very important in practice. Thus the foregoing suggests that if, for example, a high capacity road has already been built and if there is no congestion- or traffic-dependent maintenance cost, then there should be no charge for the use of the road since the marginal social costs are zero and capacity is predetermined. It is only in the very long run, when the necessity to make decisions about the standards of maintenance might effectively allow capacity to be varied, that marginal capacity costs become relevant. On the other hand, if a new major road is being planned and if the imposition of a toll would reduce the capacity required and hence the capital cost of the project, then there may be a case for imposing such a toll on the peak traffic on the basis of the long run analysis. Any advantage in doing this would naturally have to be set against the inconvenience, delay and administrative costs of collecting the toll.

There are many respects in which the simple analysis presented here is inadequate to deal with problems which occur in practice. A particular difficulty, which arises in such things as investment in port facilities and purchase of aircraft, is indivisibilities. We have assumed that quantities of capacity and their costs can be continuously varied. This has allowed us to employ the differential calculus and is a sufficiently good approximation in most cases. However, if indivisibilities are significant then techniques that rely on continuity cannot be used. Alternatives, such as integer programming, exist and the interested reader is referred to the operations research literature: a good text is Dorfman, Samuelson and Solow (1958).

Some other economic problems also arise and these are treated by, for example, Rees (1976). In particular if the demand level falls in between two widely spaced discrete units of capacity then the appropriate price will be a relatively low marginal operating cost. It may then be impossible for the revenues to cover the costs of the investment. The problem of the 'all or nothing' investment in a bridge or road mentioned above in the context of the short run analysis is a special case of this. Decisions about the desirability of investments in extra pieces of capacity and optimum facility size will then rely on some form of cost benefit evaluation of the kind discussed in chapter 8. If the investment is undertaken then the problem of how the deficit is to be financed will remain. This has been a subject of much discussion in the literature; Ruggles (1949) gives a survey.

In the case of the long run analysis and assuming that all quantities can be continuously varied, by multiplying (5.20) by x_1 and (5.21) by x_2, adding and using (5.12), which must be an equality at the optimum, we have

$$p_1 x_1 + p_2 x_2 = c_1' x_1 + c_2' x_2 + r'(K) \cdot K \qquad (5.22)$$

The left-hand side of (5.22) is the total revenue at the optimum. If the facility exhibits constant returns to scale then marginal operating and capacity costs will equal average operating and capacity costs, and so the right-hand side of (5.22) would represent total cost. The equation therefore implies that revenues would just equal costs. In other words, given constant returns to scale, the facility should be exactly self-financing if the optimum prices are charged. If there are diminishing returns to scale then marginal costs will be above average costs so that revenue will exceed costs. Conversely, if there are increasing returns to scale, the enterprise will make a loss. As a justification for railway subsidies it has been argued that there are substantial increasing returns to scale in the provision of railway capacity because of the high initial costs of providing and maintaining track and signalling.

A second source of difficulty is presented by uncertainty. In practice demand levels and responses cannot be predicted with any degree of certainty, and the life, operating costs, maintenance costs and performance of new equipment is often difficult to predict. Decision making in the presence of uncertainty is a substantial subject of its own. The way in which the analysis can be adapted to deal with the problems of uncertainty is set out in Rees (1976) and in some detail by Crew and Kleindorfer (1979).

We end this section by mentioning some studies which have applied the principles of congestion pricing and peak pricing. The first (Glaister 1976) concerns the plans in the early 1970s to build a tunnel across the English Channel to carry freight, passengers and private vehicles between England and the Continent. It was a striking example of a large planned enterprise facing an unusually severe case of peaked demand. The general strategy behind the determination of the June 1973 designs for the accompanied car traffic in the Channel tunnel seems to have been as follows. Very extensive surveys were carried out to discover the nature and determinants of current demand patterns for cross-Channel car ferry services, *at the then current fares*. The information collected included the profile of demand over the year, and the determinants of route choice and of the decision to take a foreign car holiday in a particular place for a particular length of time. Then, using predictions of changes in relevant socio-economic variables, it was possible to forecast demand behaviour in future years, but always at the same overall money crossing cost (in real terms). Using a detailed model of the behaviour of the competing shipping operators, the likely reaction of the ferries to the introduction of the tunnel at this price was predicted. This allowed the forecasting of diversion to the tunnel, and hence of total demand for its services in future years, together with a profile of demand over each year, assuming *constant prices over the year* of £19 for an average car with an average number of passengers. These demand characteristics were then used by the engineering consultants to produce the first stage designs for the terminals, rolling stock, tracks, etc. (based on 1983 or 1984 forecasts + 20%). The purpose of the following is to compare the intended design with a profit maximizing, peak pricing design.

The annual traffic forecast of 1893 kvu per direction (one kvu is one thousand vehicle units) was allocated between 17 different types of journey as displayed in table 5.1. The year

Table 5.1 Channel tunnel peak pricing results

		kvu/h	Constant prices (£)	Independent demand Price (£)	λ	Dependent demand Price (£)	λ
Holiday (July–August)							
Sat.	12–14.00 J	2.053	19	26.9	188	56.4	170
	A	1.609	19	25.6	166	56.0	172
	Day	1.533	19	25.3	968	54.8	1251
	Night	0.625	19	16.1	7.21	41.6	722
Fri., Sun.	12–14.00	1.439	19	24.9	616	48.8	593
	Day	1.211	19	23.6	1586	50.9	880
	Night	0.492	19	16.0	0	42.9	2036
Week	12–14.00	1.003	19	22.0	822	44.7	182
	Day	0.833	19	20.0	1662	45.1	8.4
	Night	0.341	19	15.7	0	45.0	0
Summer (April, May, June, September, October)							
Sat.	Day	0.492	19	19.7	0	51.0	0
	Night	0.189	19	16.0	0	46.0	0
Fri., Sun.	Day	0.398	19	16.1	0	44.5	0
	Night	0.151	19	16.0	0	43.9	0
Week	Day	0.284	19	16.1	0	29.0	0
	Night	0.106	19	16.8	0	26.9	0
Winter (November–March)		0.172	19	15.8	0	15.9	0
	Capacity (kvu/h)		2.053	0.77		0.52	
	Profit (£m)		22.537	31.228		47.195	

was split into three main periods: 'Holiday' (July and August), 'Summer' (the summer months from April to October, excluding the Holiday months) and 'Winter' (November to March). Each Holiday day was divided into 'Peak hours' (12.00 to 14.00), 'Day' (08.00 to 16.00, excluding Peak hours) and 'Night'. Summer days comprise Day and Night, and Winter operations were assumed to take place during the day only. To identify the very highest peak, Holiday Saturday Peak hours were split between July and August. Assumptions were made concerning the demand elasticities with respect to the toll charged in the different periods. In the 'independent demand' case all cross-price elasticities were assumed to be zero, whereas in the 'dependent demand' case a more complicated demand structure was used which allowed the price charged in one period to influence demand at another. Hence traffic could be switched from one period to another by adjusting price differentials, neighbouring periods being assumed to be very much closer substitutes than distant ones. The capacity costs associated with the tunnel bores themselves were assumed invariant with respect to the traffic levels, but various assumptions were made about how the costs of terminals, rolling stock, tracks, signalling and labour would be affected. Marginal capacity costs worked out at £6016 per vu per hour per annum, and marginal operating costs at £0.37 per vu per single crossing.

The most striking result in the independent demand case was that capacity fell from the 1973 design value of 2.05 to 0.77 kvu/h. Prices in the highest peak rose to £26.9 and in the winter months fell to £15.8, although the overall level of prices was broadly the same as under the constant pricing policy. The column headed λ indicates the shadow price on each constraint requiring that the demand in the respective period cannot exceed capacity — each one measures, approximately, the extra profit which could be earned if an extra unit of capacity were available during the period. Notice that they sum (approximately because of rounding) to the annual cost of providing a unit of capacity, as must be the case at the optimum. A zero value for this variable indicates that there would be excess capacity during the relevant period. Hence, although it would be profitable to have the facility underutilized much of the time, it *would* be used to capacity throughout most of the Holiday period – not just at the very highest peaks.

Profit rose from £22.5 million to £31.2 million (before deduction of fixed costs) because the fall in operating and, particularly, capacity costs made possible by reducing the size of the facility by a factor of 2.7 more than compensated for the loss in revenue from peak traffic. Notice that prices were lower in those quiet periods when there would be excess capacity under both policies, indicating that £19 was too high a price in off-peak periods. This was essentially because of the very low *marginal* operating costs.

In the dependent demand case table 5.1 shows how the extra flexibility would allow capacity to be further reduced to 0.52 kvu/h, almost one quarter of the constant price value. Consequently the overall level of prices was much higher, except in winter and the facility is fully utilized in one more period. Profit would rise to £47.2 million per annum.

This analysis was throughout on the basis of profit maximization. In the dependent demands case the peak long run marginal cost prices would have been (£0.37 + £6016/5200) or £1.53 per trip. Of course this is much less than the profit maximizing toll because of the monopoly power and price discrimination that is involved. The result would have been to operate the new, low marginal cost service in competition with, and at a higher price than, the existing high cost service.

As a second example, we turn briefly to an example of marginal social congestion cost pricing. Borins (1978) developed a model to simulate Toronto International (Malton) Airport and used it to determine marginal social cost prices of using Malton's facilities throughout the day. Table 5.2 compares the results of the optimum, marginal social cost congestion prices (MC) for different types of user of the airport, with the average cost (AC) prices (including delay costs) which users were implicitly paying in 1975. The most congested facilities were those for which the ratio of marginal to average cost prices was highest and these were the runways during the 7 to 9 am period. The terminals were less crowded than the runways, and the access roads were the least crowded. It is again apparent that there is a wide diverg-

Table 5.2 Airport facility utilization prices, 1975 summer day

Facility	Time of day	Pricing policy ($)		Units
		AC	MC	
Runway	7 am–9 am	2.20	6.56	per second
Terminal	7 am–9 am	4.99	6.25	per overseas pass
Access road	7 am–9 am	2.26	2.61	per car
Runway	9 am–4 pm	0.90	1.19	per second
Terminal	9 am–4 pm	3.81	4.31	per overseas pass
Access road	9 am–4 pm	2.07	2.18	per car
Runway	4 pm–8 pm	1.42	3.18	per second
Terminal	4 pm–8 pm	4.93	7.70	per overseas pass
Access road	4 pm–8 pm	2.33	2.69	per car
Runway	8 pm–11 pm	1.38	2.92	per second
Terminal	8 pm–11 pm	4.51	6.09	per overseas pass
Access road	8 pm–11 pm	2.21	2.47	per car

(from Borins 1978)

ence between the existing pricing strategy and one that is optimal.

Fitzgerald and Aneuryn-Evans (1973) obtain qualitatively similar results with a hypothetical example and also illustrated how the use of the 'wrong' pricing and investment rules will lead to the expansion of capacity in the face of a growing demand at the wrong time. In table 5.3 the engineers' expansion criterion is that runway expansion should take place when the number of aircraft movements exceeds three-quarters of runway capacity. The CTLA method is that used by the Commission on the Third London Airport and is based upon the minimization of the discounted sum of congestion and expansion costs. The financial method involves expansion when the increase in revenue exceeds the capital charge. These results are consistent with those obtained by Borins (1978) concerning the expansion of Malton Airport.

Table 5.3 Expansion dates (years)

Expansion criterion	Pricing rule	
	Average cost	Optimal
Engineers'	6.0	5.5
CTLA	9.2	8.6
Financial	20.2	∞
Optimal	9.6	9.0

(from Fitzgerald and Aneuryn-Evans 1973)

A further illustration of the uses of efficient congestion pricing arguments and their interrelation with decisions on investment timing will be found in the excellent account by Abelson and Flowerdew (1972) of the Commission on the Third London Airport's (Roskill) analysis of the timing of the need for the airport. We return to this point in chapter 8.

5.3 Pricing subject to financial constraint

The foregoing discussion was an example of the problem of the free choice of two (or more) price and output levels in such a way as to best serve 'the public interest' in a particular sense. However, it often happens that the straight adoption of such a policy would imply a level of subsidy for the enterprise which is unacceptably high — especially if there are large fixed costs or declining marginal costs. Alternatively it may be that a controlling agency requires a minimum level of profit from an enterprise or sector of an enterprise (an urban bus service or intercity rail travel for instance) which long run marginal cost pricing cannot be expected to produce. It then becomes necessary to think about the least damaging way of modifying the standard pricing rules. The following analysis paraphrases the definitive paper by Baumol and Bradford (1970). As they point out, the qualitative results have a long tradition in classical economics, especially in taxation theory.

Imagine, as before, an enterprise providing two services whose demands are given by $x_1 = f_1(p_1)$ and $x_2 = f_2(p_2)$; costs are given by $c_1(x_1)$ and $c_2(x_2)$. Examples might be peak and off-peak bus services or bus and rail services controlled by a common responsible authority. As in the previous section we shall choose a net willingness to pay (or the consumer surplus) objective, similar to (5.11):

$$\int_{p_1}^{\alpha_1} f_1(z) \, dz + \int_{p_2}^{\alpha_2} f_2(z) \, dz$$

$$+ p_1 x_1 + p_2 x_2 - c_1(x_1) - c_2(x_2) \quad (5.23)$$

This is to be maximized with respect to the prices subject to the constraint that the net revenue (or profit) from the enterprise must exceed some value Π:

$$p_1 x_1 + p_2 x_2 - c_1(x_1) - c_2(x_2) \geqslant R + F = \Pi \quad (5.24)$$

where R is overall required profit and F is the total of any fixed costs that may exist. There is no particular reason to assume that Π is positive. If the financing authority is willing to provide a subsidy and if fixed costs are not too high then Π may be negative so that an *operating* loss would be allowed. The problem would then be one of limiting losses, and this is perhaps the more common case in the urban transport industries.

The Lagrangian for maximization of (5.23) subject to (5.24) may be written as

$$\int_{p_1}^{\alpha_1} f_1(z) \, dz + \int_{p_2}^{\alpha_2} f_2(z) \, dz$$

$$+ (1+\lambda) [p_1 x_1 + p_2 x_2 - c_1(x_1) - c_2(x_2)] - \lambda(\Pi + S)$$

$$(5.25)$$

where $\lambda \geqslant 0$ is the Lagrangian multiplier and $S \geqslant 0$ is the slack variable, taking the value zero if the constraint is binding at the optimum. The necessary conditions for the solution are

$$-f_i(p_i) + (1+\lambda) \left(f_i + p_i \frac{df_i}{dp_i} - \frac{dc_i}{dx_i} \frac{df_i}{dp_i} \right) = 0 \quad i = 1, 2$$

$$(5.26)$$

$$S \geqslant 0; \ S = 0 \text{ if } \lambda > 0; \ S > 0 \text{ only if } \lambda = 0 \quad (5.27)$$

Equations (5.26) may be rearranged as

$$p_i - \frac{dc_i}{dx_i} = -\frac{f_i(p_i)}{df_i(p_i)/dp_i}\left(\frac{\lambda}{1+\lambda}\right) \quad i = 1, 2 \qquad (5.28)$$

or

$$\frac{p_i - dc_i/dx_i}{p_i} = -\frac{1}{\eta_i}\left(\frac{\lambda}{1+\lambda}\right) \quad i = 1, 2 \qquad (5.29)$$

where η_i is the price elasticity of demand in the ith market (which is negative). Condition (5.29) may be interpreted as saying that the proportionate deviation of price above marginal cost in each market should be inversely proportional to the respective price elasticity.

Conditions (5.29) have several implications. First note that if, at the optimum, the profit constraint is not binding then $S > 0$ and (5.27) implies that $\lambda = 0$. It follows then from (5.29) that prices will actually equal marginal costs in all markets. This is a simple restatement of the result, already obtained several times, that if the normal welfare maximizing policy will provide sufficient operating profit to satisfy the constraint in any case, then the optimum prices will be the marginal costs.

If, on the other hand, the constraint is binding, so that without it profit would be too low (or loss too high), then (5.29) implies that all prices will exceed the respective marginal costs. Further, the percentage differences will be higher in the inelastic markets. This is one reason why operators such as the railways, when fighting to contain increasing deficits, are observed to raise fares in relatively inelastic markets such as business intercity travel, whilst raising them less in markets where factors such as competition from other modes make for a relatively high effective elasticity. In other words an element of price discrimination is introduced. (It should be noted at this point that the second-order conditions for the problem require an assumption that all the price elasticities concerned are not much greater than unity in absolute value at the optimum. Otherwise an increase in price would cause a reduction in net revenue (cf. chapter 3).) The Price Commission Reports on

London Transport Fares (1978b) and on British Rail (1978a) recount examples of this.

There is yet another way of viewing (5.29). Let

$$\Delta p_i = p_i - \frac{\mathrm{d}c_i(x_i)}{\mathrm{d}x_i} \qquad (5.30)$$

be the price–marginal cost difference. Then from (5.28)

$$\Delta p_i = - \frac{f_i(p_i)}{\mathrm{d}f_i(p_i)/\mathrm{d}p_i} \left(\frac{\lambda}{1+\lambda}\right)$$

or

$$\frac{\mathrm{d}f_i(p_i)}{\mathrm{d}p_i} \Delta p_i = - f_i(p_i) \left(\frac{\lambda}{1+\lambda}\right) \quad i = 1, 2 \qquad (5.31)$$

But, if Δp_i is small it is approximately true that

$$\Delta x_i = \frac{\mathrm{d}f_i(p_i)}{\mathrm{d}p_i} \Delta p_i \quad i = 1, 2$$

where Δx_i is the change in the quantity of service i when the price is changed by some small amount from the marginal cost value. Equations (5.31) can therefore be written

$$\frac{\Delta x_i}{x_i} = - \frac{\lambda}{1+\lambda} \quad i = 1, 2 \qquad (5.32)$$

In other words the optimum price structure must have the property that the proportionate distortions in the *quantities* from what they would be if marginal cost pricing were adopted, must be the same for all markets. We know that the Pareto optimum would require marginal cost pricing. Therefore the profit constraint must produce a sub-optimum solution. The result embodied in (5.32) shows how the welfare loss associated with this sub-optimum can be minimized. It is a fundamental result and appears in various guises in the theory of indirect taxation, where the problem is to raise a given revenue whilst causing a minimum of loss of economic efficiency.

It should once again be emphasized that the results we have derived are necessary conditions for economic efficiency under constraint and do not depend for their validity on the use we have made in the exposition of consumer surplus. In fact inspection of the derivation of (5.26) shows that any social welfare function $w(p_1, p_2)$ will suffice in the argument if it has the property that

$$\partial w / \partial p_i = - f_i(p_i) \quad i = 1, 2$$

The shadow price λ has the usual interpretation as the increase in the objective attainable if the constraint is relaxed by one unit. In this context it is the extra net social welfare that would be generated at the optimum if the profit constraint were relaxed by £1. In other words it is a useful measure of the marginal social value of an extra £1 of subsidy if the operator is making a loss. Put another way, if a net profit is being required it is the net welfare loss caused by raising £1 extra profits tax, assuming the operator is pricing 'in the public interest'. A numerical example of calculations satisfying these conditions is given in section 8.3.

5.4 Non-homogeneous traffic congestion: an example of second best pricing

In section 5.3 an important simplification was made: it was assumed that the demands in the two markets were independent. In fact one would not in general expect this to be the case. Almost all goods are thought to exhibit some degree of substitutability or complementarity. Generally one would expect that different transport markets would be substitutes for each other, so that if the demand for one service were to fall because of an increase in its price then one would expect the demand for the other service to rise. In other words one would expect that

$$\partial x_i / \partial p_j > 0$$

for two substitute services. This has been confirmed in empirical studies as the work on modal split models illustrates. Similarly Fairhurst's (1975) work on London Transport bus and rail services and Lewis's (1977) work on private and public transport in London show evidence of significant substitutability.

The analysis of the previous sections can fairly easily be reworked after relaxing the restrictive assumption which essentially means that the two markets can be treated separately. The differences that this would make to the conclusions are intuitively obvious. For instance, if peak travellers respond to a fall in off-peak fares by switching time of day, then one would expect the optimum off-peak fare to be below the respective marginal cost. In this way some of the peak load can be spread to the other period with a consequent saving of expenditure on capacity. Section 3.6 illustrates an analytical approach.

The subject of this section is on rather similar lines. In section 5.1 we showed that unless a toll is imposed equilibrium will be established at a level of traffic that is above the Pareto optimum level. Suppose that in an urban setting there are actually two kinds of traffic, the private car and the publicly run bus. If there is some substitution between the modes, so that the level of car use responds to the level of bus fares and if the imposition of a road price is not feasible, then there is a case for departing from the standard long run marginal cost pricing rules in order to make some contribution towards correcting the congestion externality. There is a popular belief that this constitutes a strong argument in favour of substantial subsidy to urban public transport. However, this argument has by no means been fully accepted by governments. The theoretical case and the relevant empirical evidence for the case of London has been studied by Glaister (1974) and Glaister and Lewis (1978). The following is a simplified account of that analysis.

Let $x_1 = f_1(p_1, p_2)$ be the demand rate for private car passenger miles per unit time. This is assumed to depend upon the cost to the user of a vehicle mile, p_1, and also on the public transport fare level, p_2. Since we are to assume that a fall in bus fare will encourage a few marginal car users to switch to bus use, the two modes are substitutes and

$$\partial f_1 / \partial p_2 \geqslant 0 \qquad (5.33)$$

Similarly let $x_2 = f_2(p_1, p_2)$ be the number of passenger miles per hour demanded on the bus system. We will have

$$\partial f_2 / \partial p_2 \leqslant 0 \qquad (5.34)$$

and further, if the demand curves are compensated

$$\frac{\partial f_2}{\partial p_1} = \frac{\partial f_1}{\partial p_2} \tag{5.35}$$

(see equation (2.25)).

For the moment we take p_1 as fixed, assuming that no form of road pricing is available. The problem becomes one of choosing the bus fare p_2. We shall use the 'compensating variation' objective function developed in (2.8):

$$w(p_1, p_2) = G(\alpha_1, \alpha_2) - G(p_1, p_2) \tag{5.36}$$

where the constant arguments $\hat{p}$ and u are omitted here for clarity. This has the property that

$$\frac{\partial w(p_1, p_2)}{\partial p_2} = -f_2(p_1, p_2) \tag{5.37}$$

where the compensated demand curve is intended here. The cost of bus operations is given by $C(x_1, x_2)$ with

$$\frac{\partial C}{\partial x_1} \geqslant 0 \quad \text{and} \quad \frac{\partial C}{\partial x_2} > 0 \tag{5.38}$$

The level of car traffic x_1 appears here because if it increases it will in general increase the level of street congestion. This will slow buses down and hence increase the number of vehicles and crew required to serve a set of routes with a given level of demand for passenger miles. (The important problem of choice of service quality is treated in section 8.5 but suppressed here for simplicity.) For instance a 1 mph fall in bus speed from 5 to 4 mph would require a 20% increase in costs if carrying capacity were to be maintained. This is a significant effect in practice.

The objective for the problem may be written

$$\{G[\alpha_1, \alpha_2, f_1(\alpha_1, \alpha_2), f_2(\alpha_1, \alpha_2)]$$

$$- G[p_1, p_2, f_1(p_1, p_2), f_2(p_1, p_2)]$$

$$+ p_1 x_1 + p_2 x_2\} - p_1 x_1 - C(x_1, x_2) \tag{5.39}$$

Here the expression in braces is the willingness to pay — the sum of the compensating variation measure of consumer surplus and expenditure. It will be noted that the aggregate expenditure function $G(\cdot)$ has been modified by the inclusion of the two demand levels x_1 and x_2 (remember that $x_i = f_i(p_1, p_2)$). This is in order to represent the fact that at given prices different expenditures will be necessary to enable a consumer to attain a given level of utility if the traffic conditions differ. In other words increased traffic levels will reduce road speeds, increase journey times, inflict time losses on all travellers and therefore require an increased sum of money in compensation so as to maintain utility. Thus the terms

$$\frac{\partial G\left[p_1, p_2, f_1(p_1, p_2), f_2(p_1, p_2)\right]}{\partial x_i} > 0 \quad i = 1, 2 \quad (5.40)$$

represent the marginal social congestion costs due to a car passenger mile and a bus passenger mile respectively. They are therefore central quantities in this analysis. Because a car user generally consumes more road space than a bus user one might expect the former to exceed the latter.

The total resource costs are subtracted from the willingness to pay to give the net social benefit. It is implicit in the formulation used in (5.39) that p_1 correctly measures the true marginal resource costs (excluding congestion costs) of car use. In fact, because of the existence of taxes and many other factors this is not the case. The assumption is made for clarity, but it is a relatively simple matter to rework the following analysis with the expression $p_1 x_1$ replaced by the more general private car cost function, $h(x_1)$, say.

For the moment we are assuming that it is not feasible for some reason to use some such technique as road pricing to vary the cost to the private traveller, p_1. Hence the only choice variable is p_2. Differentiating (5.39) with respect to p_2 yields the first-order condition,

$$-f_2(p_1, p_2) - \frac{\partial G}{\partial x_1}\frac{\partial f_1}{\partial p_2} - \frac{\partial G}{\partial x_2}\frac{\partial f_2}{\partial p_2} + p_2\frac{\partial f_2}{\partial p_2} + f_2(p_1, p_2)$$

$$-\frac{\partial C}{\partial x_1}\frac{\partial f_1}{\partial p_2} - \frac{\partial C}{\partial x_2}\frac{\partial f_2}{\partial p_2} = 0$$

This simplifies considerably to

$$p_2 = \left(\frac{\partial C}{\partial x_2} + \frac{\partial G}{\partial x_2}\right) + \left(\frac{\partial C}{\partial x_1} + \frac{\partial G}{\partial x_1}\right) \frac{\partial f_1/\partial p_2}{\partial f_2/\partial p_2}$$

or equivalently

$$p_2 = \left(\frac{\partial C}{\partial x_2} + \frac{\partial G}{\partial x_2}\right) + \left(\frac{\partial C}{\partial x_1} + \frac{\partial G}{\partial x_1}\right) \frac{x_1 \eta_{12}}{x_2 \eta_{22}} \qquad (5.41)$$

where η_{12} is the cross-price elasticity of private travel with respect to the bus fare, and η_{22} is the own-price elasticity of bus demand. The expressions in parentheses in (5.41) are the respective marginal social costs of travel by the two modes, each composed of the direct effect on the cost of bus operations and the time loss costs due to congestion. In view of (5.38) and (5.40) all the terms involved in the parentheses are positive. Because of (5.33) η_{12} will be positive, but η_{22} will be negative. We can now interpret (5.41): it says that at the optimum the bus fare should equal the marginal social cost of a bus passenger mile, reduced by the subtraction of a certain factor. The magnitude of this 'discount' will depend upon several things: the marginal social cost of private car use (over and above the simple resource costs), the responsiveness of car use to the level of bus fares and the level of car demand relative to bus demand. It seems reasonable that the modification to the difference between bus fare and bus marginal social cost should depend on each of these factors in the way that (5.41) suggests. Note that if there is no response by car users to changes in bus fares then the rule of marginal social cost pricing is restored, because lowering bus fares will then achieve nothing in the way of alleviating the economic inefficiency in the private transport sector caused by uncontrolled congestion. Similarly, marginal social cost pricing will emerge if x_1 is zero or if the marginal social cost of car use is zero, since in either of these cases there is no problem in the private car sector.

This is a simple example of what has become known as *the theory of the second best* (see Lipsey and Lancaster 1956).

The proposition can be stated in considerable generality, but a simple statement of the main idea is as follows. Suppose that for some reason or another there is a market for a commodity where a 'price distortion' exists in the sense that the price charged is different from that which the conditions of economic efficiency would require. Suppose also that for some reason it is not possible for an administrative agency to intervene to compel a correction of the distortion, but that it does have some influence over the pricing of some other commodities (typically these would be the outputs of some public enterprise). Then if the pricing of these other commodities will influence the demand conditions in the distorted market (because, say, they are substitutes or complements) then there is a case for deliberately distorting prices of these other commodities. In this way a second best optimum can be achieved although the best of all possible worlds cannot be achieved.

The interested reader will find it easy to confirm that the 'first best' solution to the problem would involve marginal cost pricing on both modes, as one would expect in view of the material in sections 5.1 to 5.3. This is done by assuming that a form of road pricing is after all feasible so that p_1 becomes a choice variable for the authorities. It is then a matter of maximizing (5.39) with respect to both prices. In this case the externality in the private transport sector can be 'internalized' by the imposition of road tax so that the case for manipulating bus fares is removed.

We have emphasized throughout this chapter that the results that we have derived concerning economic efficiency do not rely on the validity of consumer surplus techniques which have been used here as an expository device. It will be noted that we have at no point actually evaluated consumer surplus — we have simply derived necessary conditions for it to be maximized in the knowledge that it is one example of a social welfare function so that our conditions are necessary for economic efficiency. The qualitative results obtained in the present section may be derived alternatively from 'first principles', using the arguments expounded by Malinvaud (1972) and Sherman (1971).

5.5 The integration of second best with peak pricing: an example

It has been the view of recent UK governments that the objectives discussed in the previous section can be more readily achieved by means of traffic management and other techniques than by the grant of subsidy to public transport operators.

For example, the UK Transport Policy White Paper (1977, paragraph 58) says that 'it is sometimes argued that subsidies should be paid to public transport to attract travellers out of cars and so reduce congestion on the roads.... The evidence is that there are few places where [the necessary] conditions are met and that subsidies paid for this reason are, on the whole, misplaced'.

As we have shown the validity of this conclusion turns on the actual magnitudes of the marginal social costs of car use, and of the cross-price elasticities between the modes. In London there are three principal modes of transport: private vehicle, bus and rail. The situation is further complicated by the fact that the available evidence indicates that own- and cross-price elasticities, as well as marginal costs, differ very significantly between the peak and the off-peak. Thus the possibilities of transferring trips between periods as well as between modes means that an adequate treatment of even a highly aggregate and simplistic system will require consideration of the three modes and peak and off-peak times of day.

Glaister and Lewis (1978) collected the best evidence available on demand responses and social costs for the three competing modes (omitting the important taxi mode) in the Greater London area. Taking into account the differences between peak and off-peak conditions they attempted to integrate this evidence into a simplistic general equilibrium system. The aim was to explore the prices and subsidy levels implied by the peak pricing and second best considerations outlined in sections 5.2 and 5.4 to see if there is any substance in the 'congestion reducing' arguments against charging public transport users their full marginal costs.

The results are displayed in table 5.4 (in 1977 prices). This gives the marginal costs used, the computed optimum fares, the 'subsidies' in £ per hour to each of the modes, the resulting rates of traffic flow, the ratios of flow rates to subsidy rates in passenger miles per £ and the total annual subsidy assuming a five-day week and a 52-week year. Calculations were carried out with two sets of operating cost data: case 1 is intended to represent estimates of short run marginal costs (including social costs), while in case 2 some allowance is made for the marginal capacity costs of an extra passenger mile. On the basis of information on speed–flow relationships and time values, we assumed that the marginal social cost of a peak passenger mile would decline linearly from £0.15 at current traffic levels to £0.11 at half that level. The corresponding figure for a peak bus passenger mile was taken to be a constant £0.05.

The 'subsidies' referred to in table 5.4 are subsidies on operating costs, so fixed costs would require additional subsidy. Since marginal operating costs are assumed constant they are also average operating costs so that a price equal to marginal operating cost will imply a zero operating subsidy. It should be noted that in case 1 marginal capacity costs are not allocated to peak users so that they are being implicitly treated as fixed costs and therefore do not appear in the calculation of the 'subsidies' for case 1. The 'passenger miles per £' figure is quoted because this statistic is currently used as a measure of performance for management purposes by the London Transport Executive (see Quarmby 1977, and chapter 8 where the objective is discussed in detail). The results for case 1 illustrate the substantial gap between computed optimum fares and assumed marginal costs. It will be noted that in this case marginal costs for rail are considerably below those for bus, which explains the rather low peak and off-peak rail fares of 0.3 and 0.6 pence. The highest rate of subsidy is to peak rail and this achieves a doubling of peak rail traffic and a quadrupling of off-peak rail traffic, whilst reducing both car and bus traffic. Such an increase in peak rail traffic would be infeasible in practice, but the result is a consequence of failing to allocate true marginal capacity costs to peak rail users. The overall subsidy level, neglecting capacity costs, for a five day week would be £112 million per annum. It is interesting to note that the assumed cost structure here is such that it is optimum to have a peak rail fare

Table 5.4 Costs, fares and subsidies for London

Case	Marginal costs (pence per passenger mile)				Fares (pence per passenger mile)			
	Bus		Rail		Bus		Rail	
	Peak	Off-peak	Peak	Off-peak	Peak	Off-peak	Peak	Off-peak
Present					4.3	4.3	4.3	4.3
1	11	6	2	1	3.4	3.1	0.3	0.5
2	14	6	30	1	5.22	2.21	20.4	0.39
3	14	6	10	1	7.02	3.12	6.11	0.54

Case	Subsidies ($£$ per hour $\times 10^4$)				Traffic flows (passengers per hour $\times 10^6$)				
	Bus		Rail		Car	Bus		Rail	
	Peak	Off-peak	Peak	Off-peak		Peak	Off-peak	Peak	Off-peak
Present					1.46	0.7	0.18	1.76	0.22
1	1.35	0.36	5.89	0.42	1.25	0.51	0.13	3.53	0.86
2	2.97	0.64	104	0.73	1.59	0.79	0.17	1.08	1.20
3	1.20	0.39	6.35	0.45	1.50	0.60	0.14	1.63	0.97

Case	Passenger miles (per $£$ subsidy)				Total annual subsidy ($£ \times 10^6$)
	Bus		Rail		
	Peak	Off-peak	Peak	Off-peak	
Present					
1	38	35	60	207	137
2	26	26	10	164	251
3	50	35	26	218	144

below the off-peak fare in spite of it having double the marginal cost.

The allocation of marginal capacity costs to peak users in case 2 results in an increase of peak marginal social bus costs from 11 pence to 14 pence and a substantial increase of peak rail costs from 6 pence to 30 pence. Compared with case 1 this leads to a modest increase in peak bus fares (although they remain only one half of marginal costs) and an increase in explicit subsidy to this mode. Peak rail fares rise substantially, but only to three-quarters of their allocated costs. Both off-peak fares fall because of the increased advantage in attracting public transport traffic out of the peak. This fares structure would cause a 9% increase in car traffic, a 13% increase in peak bus traffic, a decrease in off-peak bus traffic, a substantial decline in peak rail traffic and a large increase in off-peak rail traffic. Peak rail traffic attracts a large subsidy which pushes the total subsidy up to £159 million per annum. In respect of peak rail marginal costs cases 1 and 2 represent extreme positions. As a compromise results of a case 3 are presented, which is as for case 2, except that peak rail costs are reduced to 10 pence per passenger mile. This would seem to be the most reasonable case. It would suggest an increase of peak fares from 4.3 pence to 7.0 pence but a reduction of off-peak bus fares to 3.1 pence. Similarly peak rail fares would be increased to 6.1 pence but off-peak rail fares reduced substantially to about 0.5 pence. This would lead to a very marginal increase in car use, a 17% fall in peak bus traffic, slight falls in off-peak bus and peak rail traffic and a four-and-a-half fold increase in off-peak rail traffic. The overall subsidy level would be about £144 million per annum, 69% of which would be attributable to peak rail services.

Within the limited validity of the method and the data, we found that whatever view one takes about the allocation of marginal capacity costs there is a defensible case for a subsidy to the operation of public transport, but that this would be unlikely to exceed, say, £150 million per annum (for a five-day week) for the whole system in addition to a subsidy to cover fixed costs. The solutions are dominated by the marginal cost of the modes and, insofar as rail has a lower marginal cost than bus, the results would suggest some advantage in a general lowering of rail fares relative to bus fares in order to encourage some redistribution of traffic to the cheaper mode. A differential of 4 to 5 pence per passenger mile between peak and off-peak on both modes is indicated. It is quite possible that one could make a case for free off-peak transport if that would allow significant cost savings through the avoidance of collection costs which we have not considered. Current private car traffic levels and overall subsidy levels are quite close to the optimum calculated from our case 3.

A quite different argument is that economic efficiency is not the only consideration and that an equally valid reason for subsidy is that public transport is generally used by the relatively poor and that a measure of income redistribution can be achieved in this way. On the other hand it can be argued that this is not a particularly effective method of income redistribution, and in any case there is some dispute about whether the poor do predominate in public transport use. It is said that many urban public transport users are in fact car owners and that it is well known that the rich travel further and more often than the poor. The case becomes even more doubtful if transport subsidy has to be financed by form of taxation, such as property taxes, which may themselves be regressive in their incidence. Grey (1975) gives a detailed discussion of this question, but it seems likely that it will be some time before sufficient data become available to resolve this issue.

A further strong argument against subsidy, whatever its justification, is that it removes the incentives to production efficiency — and possibly some of the mechanisms for scrutiny and information collection as well — from the management structure. The consequent wastage of resources and possible inability to contain the level of subsidy greatly outweighs any advantages the subsidy might bring. It is for this kind of reason that London Transport management have adopted the corporate aim 'of maximizing passenger miles subject to financial constraint' which is discussed in chapter 8. The relative merits of the arguments in favour of striving to achieve economically efficient prices as against striving to eliminate incompetence and waste has become known as the

'X-inefficiency debate' (see Leibenstein 1966 and Pryke 1977).
We return to this in chapter 9.

5.6 Problems

(1) In a certain congested street the speed of homogeneous
vehicles v miles per hour, is given by

$$v = 20,000/x$$

where x is the flow of vehicle miles per hour. The generalized
cost g of a vehicle mile is the sum of the operating cost of
£0.1 per vehicle mile and the cost of time taken, valued at
£2 per vehicle hour. The demand for vehicle miles is given by

$$x = 5000 - 10,000g$$

(a) What is the equilibrium rate of flow?
(b) What rate of tax per vehicle mile would you impose?
     Give a justification of your answer and discuss the
     general principles and practicability of taxation of this
     kind.

(2) Each vehicle in a homogeneous traffic flow moving in a
congested street incurs a generalized cost of g pence per mile,
given by

$$g = c(q) + t$$

where t is a tax, q is the traffic flow and $c(q)$ represents additional private costs due to congestion. The demand for the
use of the road is given by

$$q = f(g)$$

Derive and interpret an expression for the optimum rate of
tax, and show that if

$$c(q) = q^\alpha \quad f(g) = g^{-\epsilon} \qquad \alpha > 0, \epsilon > 0$$

then the optimum rate of tax is given by

$$t = \alpha(1 + \alpha)^{-\alpha\epsilon/(1 + \alpha\epsilon)}$$

(3) A *profit maximizing* enterprise wishes to design a new
urban railway. It is known that there will be a 'rush hour'

lasting t_1 hours and a 'normal' period lasting t_2 hours during each day, and that the demand rates per hour will be given by

$$q_1 = \alpha_0 + \alpha_1 p_1 + \alpha_2 p_2$$
$$q_2 = \beta_0 + \beta_1 p_1 + \beta_2 p_2$$

respectively, where p_1 and p_2 are the fares charged in the two periods. The cost of carrying a demand rate of q people per hour for t hours is given by γtq and the daily interest and maintenance cost of providing the capacity to carry K people per hour is given by ρK.

(a) Derive expressions for the two optimum fares in terms of the parameters of the problem.

(b) Simplify these results in the special case where $\alpha_2 = \beta_1 = 0$, and discuss the economic interpretation and implications of the results, including consideration of the case where $\gamma = 0$.

(c) Discuss briefly why the results in the general case are different from those obtained in the special case under (b). How would you expect these fares to be modified if the service were to be run in the 'public interest'?

(4) Suppose there are k identical individuals in a city, each having a gross income of m. Suppose they each consume a quantity z of consumption good, a quantity x_r of private transport and a quantity x_u of public transport. The utility function of each consumer is:

$$z^\alpha x_r^\beta x_u^\gamma \qquad \alpha + \beta + \gamma = 1$$

and the goods have prices $1, p_r, p_u$ respectively. Each citizen pays income tax to the city council at rate t, so his budget constraint is:

$$z + p_r x_r + p_u x_u = m - t$$

Show that each citizen will consume $\alpha(m - t)$ of consumption good, $\beta(m - t)/p_r$ of private transport and $\gamma(m - t)/p_u$ of public transport. Hence show that the maximum utility attained by each consumer is:

$$U^* = \alpha^\alpha \beta^\beta \gamma^\gamma (m - t)/p_r^\beta p_u^\gamma$$

Now suppose that the city council provides the public transport and spends its entire tax revenue kt to make up the rest of the costs, given by $kC(x_u, x_r)$. Thus:

$$t = C(x_u, x_r) - p_u x_u$$

Assume that the city council wishes to maximize the sum of the utilities of its population.

Discuss the relationship of optimum prices to marginal costs, and the practical implications, in cases:

(a) the council can vary only p_u and t; and
(b) the council can vary p_u, t and p_r.

(5) Suppose that British Rail can identify two distinct passenger markets: commuting and intercity. The passenger miles demanded on the two services are known to be given by

$$x_1 = \alpha_1 p_1^{\beta_1} \quad \text{and} \quad x_2 = \alpha_2 p_2^{\beta_2}$$

where $-1 < \beta_1 < 0$ but $\beta_2 < -1$.

The fares are £p_1 and £p_2 per passenger mile; β_1 and β_2 are constants. Operating costs are £$c_1 x_1$ and £$c_2 x_2$, where c_1 and c_2 are constants.

Central government makes a grant towards fixed costs but stipulates that British Rail should earn sufficient profit on its operations to make a contribution of £$\pi > 0$ to fixed costs. At what level should fares be fixed? How does the resulting fare structure compare with current actual practice, and what objections would you anticipate to any changes suggested by your analysis? On what basis might British Rail argue in favour of an increased subsidy, and what can be said about the case where $\pi = 0$?

(6) 'In principle the problem of economically efficient pricing and investment decisions for urban public transport systems can be treated separately from the problem of congestion of private vehicles in the street. In practice this has not been achieved and effects on road traffic are a major consideration in public transport planning'. Give a rigorous evaluation of this statement. How would you estimate the practical importance of your arguments?

6 Queues

Queues are a commonplace feature of travel by any mode. There are clearly substantial gains to be had from the efficient design of facilities which have to cope with them. The literature on queues is vast, still growing and very complex. An example of a good text is Cox and Smith (1961). The intention here is to expound the theory of the simplest possible type of queue to illustrate that there are certain intrinsic features of stochastic processes which cannot always be assumed to be insignificant. This adds an extra complication to the deterministic theory which we have developed in the preceding chapters.

6.1 Random processes

By way of a preliminary we must define and analyse what we mean by a purely random process. A fundamental notion is that of an *event*. A suitable definition of an event will often be obvious from the context of the problem: for instance, if we were studying the behaviour of queues of fares at a taxi rank then one event would be the arrival of a new fare at the end of the queue; another would be the service of the person at the head of the queue by the arrival of a taxi to take him to his destination. We say that events are occurring *at random* (or according to a Poisson process) if the probability of one event occurring in any short time interval Δt is independent of the past history of the process; in particular it must be independent of whether an event has just occurred.

In practice this condition is very rarely strictly satisfied. If we arrive at a bus stop hoping to catch a bus on an unscheduled service, and we see that we have just missed a bus then we tend to moderate our expectations as to whether another bus will appear within the next few seconds. The arrival of buses is not, therefore, seen as a random process. Similarly it has been observed that the arrival of vehicles at a certain point of a motorway is not always random, because of the phenomenon of 'platooning'. Thus, whilst the assumption of pure randomness is convenient as a simplification which preserves some of the essential features of the subject, and which may be valid in some cases as an approximation, it can be seriously misleading in other cases. The problem of optimum phasing of traffic lights at interacting junctions in a network would be one example, where very much more complicated models are required.

Consider random arrivals at some facility at an *average arrival rate* λ per unit time. By this we mean that $\lambda \Delta t$ is approximately the probability of one arrival in the short interval Δt. In other words we assume that the probability of an arrival is proportional to the length of the time interval and independent of what has happened in the preceding period. Note that this assumption is valid if, but only if, the interval Δt is short. For example, if arrivals are occurring at random at the average rate of six per hour then the probability of one arrival in any minute will be approximately $6 \times 1/60$, or $1/10$.

Let $P_n(t)$ be the probability that n arrivals have occurred after a period of length t. The object is to find an expression for this in terms of λ, n and t. Suppose first that $n \neq 0$. Then n arrivals at t would have occurred either if there had been n arrivals at $t - \Delta t$ and none in Δt, or if there had been $n - 1$ at $t - \Delta t$ and one arrival in Δt:

$$P_n(t) = P_n(t - \Delta t)(1 - \lambda \Delta t) + P_{n-1}(t - \Delta t)\lambda \Delta t$$

$$(6.1)$$

This may be rewritten

$$\frac{P_n(t) - P_n(t - \Delta t)}{\Delta t} = -\lambda P_n(t - \Delta t) + \lambda P_{n-1}(t - \Delta t)$$

$$(6.2)$$

The numerator on the left-hand side of (6.2) is the change in the function $P_n(t)$ during the interval Δt. Dividing by Δt yields the *rate* of change, and taking the limit as Δt becomes indefinitely small gives what is by definition the derivative:

$$\frac{dP_n(t)}{dt} = -\lambda P_n(t) + \lambda P_{n-1}(t) \tag{6.3}$$

In particular if $n = 1$ (6.3) becomes

$$\frac{dP_1(t)}{dt} = \lambda[P_0(t) - P_1(t)] \tag{6.4}$$

However, in order to obtain an expression for $P_0(t)$ in (6.4), suppose that $n = 0$. Then the second term on the right-hand side of (6.1) must be deleted. An argument analogous to that leading to (6.3) then gives:

$$\frac{dP_0(t)}{dt} = -\lambda P_0(t) \tag{6.5}$$

This is an elementary differential equation with the solution

$$P_0(t) = k\,e^{-\lambda t}$$

as can be confirmed by substitution in (6.5). But it must be the case that $P_0(0) = 1$, implying that $k = 1$. Substituting now for $P_0(t)$ in (6.4) gives:

$$\frac{dP_1(t)}{dt} = \lambda[e^{-\lambda t} - P_1(t)] \tag{6.6}$$

This has solution

$$P_1(t) = \lambda t\,e^{-\lambda t} \tag{6.7}$$

Putting $n = 2$ in (6.3) and eliminating $P_1(t)$ from (6.7),

$$\frac{dP_2(t)}{dt} = \lambda[\lambda t\,e^{-\lambda t} - P_2(t)]$$

with solution

$$P_2(t) = \tfrac{1}{2}(\lambda t)^2\,e^{-\lambda t}$$

Repeating this process recursively gives the solution for $P_n(t)$

which we were seeking:

$$P_n(t) = \frac{(\lambda t)^n \, e^{-\lambda t}}{n!} \qquad (6.8)$$

where $n! = n(n-1)(n-2)\ldots 2.1$. Equation (6.8) defines a probability distribution in n for each value of t which is known as the Poisson distribution. It is fundamental to the theory of random processes. To take our earlier example with an average arrival rate of six per hour, the probability of exactly one arrival during 10 minutes is e^{-1} or 0.37. Similarly the probability of two arrivals in 10 minutes is $\frac{1}{2}e^{-1}$ or 0.18, and the probability of one arrival in half an hour is

$$\frac{(6 \cdot \frac{1}{2})^1 \, c^{-6 \cdot 1/2}}{1} = 0.15$$

An important special case is given when $n = 0$. We then have

$$P_0(t) = e^{-\lambda t} \qquad (6.9)$$

This is the probability of having to wait longer than t for the first occurrence of the first event. In our example, the probability of no arrivals after half an hour is e^{-3}, or 0.05. This is obviously a quantity of some importance to the potential passenger of a random bus service. It is unlikely that he would have to wait as long as half an hour, although he *might* have to wait longer. A somewhat more informative quantity would be the probability distribution function of the waiting time. Equation (6.9) gives the probability of having to wait at least t before the occurrence of the first event. Letting u represent the random variable, 'waiting time to the first event', the cumulative distribution function is therefore given by

$$F(u) = \text{Probability } (u < t)$$
$$= 1 - e^{-\lambda t}$$

Hence the density function is

$$f(u) = \lambda \, e^{-\lambda t}$$

This is the *negative exponential distribution* and it always characterizes the waiting time for random processes. Besides

representing the waiting time for the first event, it also
applies to the time between any two events and to the next
event at any arbitrarily selected instant. This is obvious
because there is no distinction between these quantities in
view of the definition of a random process. It is easily shown
that the distribution has the mean $1/\lambda$ and variance $1/\lambda^2$. It is
to be expected that a higher arrival rate would mean a lower
average waiting time and a lower variability of waiting times.

Returning to the general Poisson distribution in (6.8), the
mean is λt and the variance is equal to the mean; again, this
is what would be expected. The average number of arrivals
must increase in direct proportion to the elapsed time and
the variability of that total must also increase with time.

6.2 General queues

The specification of any queueing process involves three
essential elements: the *input process*, the *queue discipline*
and the *service mechanism*. The input process is a description
of the way in which customers arrive at the facility, including
a specification of the stochastic process involved. This might
be a constant, deterministic flow, a Poisson process or some
other stochastic process.

The queue discipline specifies various features of the way
in which the queue is handled. It will specify if the 'first
come first served' rule is to be observed, whether a potential
queuer can decide against queueing if the queue is too long,
and what the rules are if there are several queues.

The service mechanism specifies the distribution of service
times – the constant and Poisson are the simplest cases. It
will also specify the number of servers.

A queue is said to be in equilibrium, if *on the average the
number being served is equal to the number arriving at the
queue*, so that the expected queue length is a constant. To
deal only with equilibrium theory is a convenient and major
simplification. The results quoted here only apply to equilibrium but it is important to be aware that there are many
situations where it is quite inappropriate. An example would
be the modelling of the build-up of queues at road junctions
during relatively short peak periods. Here the flow rate will

build up to the point where a junction becomes saturated and cannot serve the flow of vehicles wishing to use it. The queue will then start to grow and at these rates would continue to do so indefinitely. However, the peak of the rush hour passes and the arrival rate of vehicles eventually falls below the rate at which they can be served by the junction. The queue will then dwindle away. It is fairly clear that the use of equilibrium theory to estimate total delays in a situation like this might be misleading and that it is quite possible that a deterministic model would be much more satisfactory for the purpose. This is reflected in the recent versions of COBA, the UK Department of Transport's official method of road investment appraisal where a simple deterministic model replaces the equilibrium queueing results of the earlier versions (Department of Transport 1980).

There are three quantities of particular interest in a queue which has reached equilibrium: the number of individuals in the queue (the expected queue length), the average waiting times and the distribution of the queue length. We shall now give statements of each of these without proofs. They are standard and may be found in many suitable texts; Bailey (1964) gives a useful short summary.

Let the random variable V represent the time taken for a customer to be served. Denote its mean by $E(V)$ and its variance by σ_V^2. Then the mean number of arrivals during $E(V)$ is known as the *traffic intensity* and it is denoted by ρ. This is a fundamental quantity. For example, if arrivals are random at the rate of five per hour and services are also random at six per hour then ρ would be $5/6$.

Suppose that the input process is Poisson with parameter λ whilst the service process is for the moment unspecified. Then if $E(Q)$ is the expected queue length in equilibrium it is given by

$$E(Q) = \frac{\rho(2 - \rho) + \lambda^2 \sigma_V^2}{2(1 - \rho)} \tag{6.10}$$

As would be expected (6.10) shows that for a given traffic intensity and arrival rate, the expected queue length will increase with the variance of the service time. This illustrates a recurring point: that for a *given* mean service capability *variability* of service times reduces the efficiency of the facility and increases the queue length. This is one of the features of the random nature of the process which cannot be adequately captured by deterministic models. As we shall see it is related to the fact that there is always a finite probability of a queue being empty for a while so that the server is standing idle.

The other main point to note about (6.10) is that if it is to make any sense then it is necessary that

$$\rho < 1 \qquad\qquad (6.11)$$

in other words that the arrival rate be strictly less than the service rate. As the arrival rate approaches the service rate the traffic intensity approaches unity and the equilibrium queue length becomes unbounded. This is because there will inevitably be periods when the queue is empty and the server is idle and it becomes increasingly more difficult for the server to 'catch up' during the complimentary periods of unusually heavy demand. If both arrival and service processes were deterministic and equal then one could obviously attain equilibrium with no queue at all. But if either of the processes exhibited any variability then a queue would build up indefinitely.

6.3 Special cases

It was assumed in deriving (6.10) that the arrival process was a Poisson process, but no assumption was made about the service process. Let us now assume that this exhibits negative exponential service times: in other words that it is also a random process with parameter μ. By the definition of ρ we have

$$\rho = \lambda E(V)$$

Since the mean of the service time distribution in this case is $1/\mu$ we therefore have

$$\rho = \lambda/\mu$$

or

$$1/\mu = \rho/\lambda \qquad\qquad (6.12)$$

Also, we know that

$$\sigma_V^2 = 1/\mu^2$$

and so from (6.12)

$$\sigma_V^2 = \rho^2/\lambda^2$$

Substituting in (6.10) for σ_V^2 then reduces the expression for the queue length to

$$E(Q) = \frac{\rho}{1 - \rho} \qquad (6.13)$$

To take our earlier example, if passengers arrive at a cab rank at random at five per hour and cabs arrive at random every ten minutes then $\rho = 5/6$ and the average queue will contain five individuals. Perhaps a more interesting quantity to the economist would be the expected waiting time for the individual joining the queue; we shall come to this in section (6.4). Incidentally, it would be very misleading to use such a simplistic model of queueing for taxis in some situations; passengers may not arrive at random because, say, of the arrival of a train-load of passengers at a railway terminus. Also they may be much more likely to join a short queue than a long one, thus destroying the implicit assumption that the arrival rate is independent of the state of the queue. Similarly more taxis may be attracted by a long queue than a short one. Finally there may be several alternative places to which the potential fare might go in the attempt to catch a taxi, thus falsifying the assumption that there is a single channel of service.

As a second special case assume that the service time is a constant whilst the arrival process is again random. Then $\sigma_V^2 = 0$ and (6.10) reduces to

$$E(Q) = \frac{\rho(2 - \rho)}{2(1 - \rho)} \qquad (6.14)$$

which is obviously less than (6.10).

6.4 Waiting times

Accepting that time has a value, the decision to join a queue must be related to the time that the individual must expect to wait in it. Thus the behaviour of waiting times is of as much interest as that of queue lengths. In fact several studies have recently claimed to have established that the value travellers place on a unit reduction of waiting time is substantially higher than the corresponding figure for walking or in-vehicle time (see section 7.4 below).

The general waiting time formula corresponding to (6.10) is given by

$$E(W) = \frac{\rho^2 + \lambda^2 \sigma_V^2}{2\lambda(1 - \rho)} \qquad (6.15)$$

this being the waiting time that any one customer would expect to suffer on average. If negative exponential service times are assumed then this reduces to

$$E(W) = \frac{\rho^2}{\lambda(1 - \rho)} \qquad (6.16)$$

We showed earlier that with random arrivals of passengers at a cab rank at a rate of five per hour, and random arrivals of cabs every ten minutes on average then and the average queue length would be five individuals. The average waiting time given by (6.16) would then be $(5/6)^2/(5 \cdot 1/6)$ which is 5/6 hours or 50 minutes. Note that if the arrival and service rates increase in proportion, so that ρ is unchanged then the average waiting time falls, although the average queue length will be unchanged as (6.13) shows. This is natural since the speed of passage down the queue has increased. In the context of bus queues Mohring (1972) observed that this represents a kind of scale benefit. If the number of travellers doubles and the service frequency doubles so as to maintain a constant queue length, then the costs might be expected to roughly double. But each pre-existing traveller now has to queue for half as long as before, and so receives an external benefit.

If variance of the service times can be eliminated, so that the service time is a constant, then (6.15) immediately reduces to:

$$E(W) = \frac{\rho^2}{2\lambda(1 - \rho)} \qquad (6.17)$$

This is precisely one half of the previous expression. Thus, with random arrivals, if random services can be rendered constant then the waste due to queuing delays can be halved. It should be noted that this rather remarkable result is achieved without increasing the nominal capacity of the service facility, but only by reducing the variability of services. That the queuing costs increase with the variability of service times when the process is other than random can easily be seen from the general formula (6.15).

Perhaps the most relevant quantity from the point of view of economic assessment of the costs of queuing is the value of the man hours wasted in each hour. This is the product of the money value of an hour of time with the queue length. If it was necessary to appraise a proposal to invest so as to reduce waiting times then it would be necessary to calculate the expected reduction in this value. The field of estimating values to be attributed to marginal savings of time for transport users is discussed in section 7.4.

In our example, anything which induced one more cab arrival an hour so that there were seven per hour, would reduce the expected queue length to $2\frac{1}{2}$ people, a saving of $2\frac{1}{4}$ hours per hour. This, multiplied by a value of one hour's saved time, would be the maximum hourly payment that it would be worth making in order to secure the improvement in service.

6.5 The distribution of the queue length and waiting times

So far we have simply been concerned with the means of two distributions. But queue length and waiting times are random variables and the means of their probability distributions, whilst of considerable interest, fail to convey some important information. For example, one may wish to know the probability that the queue will be empty so as to estimate the availability of the server for rest, maintenance or other tasks. Similarly one may wish to know the probability that the number in the queue will exceed some given number if space or other facilities have to be provided for the individuals or vehicles in the queue. From the point of view of the user, the mean waiting time may not be very relevant: he may be much more concerned with the probability of having to wait more than a certain time in the queue, because, say, that would make him late for an appointment.

Expressions in the general case are complicated, but in our special case of random arrivals and services the distribution of queue length left behind by a departing customer is given by:

$$p_r = (1 - \rho) \rho^r \qquad (6.18)$$

where p_r is the probability that there will be r individuals in the queue at any chosen instant. In particular, note that $p_0 = (1 - \rho)$ which gives the probability that the queue will be empty. Thus our taxi queue will be empty for 1/6 of the time. Its mean length is 5; the probability that it will be twice as long is $(1 - \rho) \rho^{10}$, or 0.027. The probability of a zero waiting time is obviously $(1 - \rho)$. If waiting time is not zero then its distribution is a negative exponential:

$$\rho (\mu - \lambda) \exp [-(\mu - \lambda) W] \qquad (6.19)$$

Hence the probability of having to wait longer than W^* is

$$\rho \exp [-(\mu - \lambda) W^*]$$

With W^* equal to the mean of 5/6 hours this gives 0.36. The probability of having to wait one hour or longer is 0.31 and the probability of having to wait five minutes or longer is 0.77. There is always a probability of 1/6 that the queue will be empty and therefore waiting time will be zero.

6.6 Airport runway capacity: an example

An example of the application of principles similar to those outlined in this chapter is provided by the calculations of runway capacity carried out for the Commission on the Third London Airport (Roskill) and described by Abelson and Flowerdew (1972). They describe how the capacity of a single runway handling arrivals and departures varies with the ratio of arrivals to departures and also depends on the separation between successive aircraft. The theoretical hourly rate for landing and take-off can be calculated, assuming full utilization of the runways; this is shown in table 6.1. It will

Table 6.1 Runway capacity

Arrival/departure ratio	Aircraft movements per hour		
	Theoretical capacity	Practical capacity	Utilization (%)
0.8	65	42	65
1.0	72	42	58
1.2	61	41	67

Source: Abelson and Flowerdew (1972)

be noted that theoretical capacity increases as the ratio of arrivals to departures tends to one, because the spacings between landing and take-off, or take-off and landing, are less than the spacings between consecutive landings and consecutive take-offs. However, in practice aircraft will arrive for landings and be ready for take-offs at irregular intervals. There is therefore always the possibility that there is no aircraft wanting to use the runway when it becomes vacant. This can only be avoided by having considerable queues of aircraft waiting to take off and waiting to land; otherwise the theoretical capacity cannot be attained. The amount of traffic that can in fact be handled without excessive delay (defined arbitrarily as an average delay over four minutes) can be calculated and is shown in table 6.1. It will be noted that the reduction in effective capacity which is due to the randomness of arrivals and departures is between 33% and 42%.

It was estimated that 'computer assisted approach sequencing', which would help to regulate arrivals, would be able to raise London (Heathrow) Airport's capacity by 10%.

Another phenomenon due to queuing is the increase in the variance in total flying time: this may mean that a greater margin of fuel has to be carried, with its attendant weight penalty, and schedules have to be adjusted in a way that gives a poorer effective aircraft utilization. Both these effects imply higher costs for the airlines. It was further suggested to the Commission that there would be very high costs to passengers for being late and so it would be better to err by being early — and hence better to expand airport capacity earlier rather than later.

6.7 Problems

(1) If individuals are arriving at some service facility at rate λ according to a random (Poisson) process, derive the distributions of the numbers who have arrived after some interval t and of the time between arrivals.

At a particular stop on a certain bus route individuals arrive at random at the rate of 18 per hour and buses arrive at random every three minutes on average. Each bus can pick up exactly one passenger.

(a)　What percentage of the time is the bus queue empty?
(b)　How long is the queue expected to be on average?
(c)　What is the average waiting time in the queue?
(d)　Discuss the considerations you consider relevant to the decision to change the service quality by altering the service frequency or by other means.

(2) Individuals arrive at random at a ticket office at the mean rate of 100 individuals per hour. Service times are exponentially distributed with a mean time of $\frac{1}{2}$ minute. What are the expected queue length and expected waiting time? A publicity campaign is proposed at a cost of $£\frac{7}{48}$ per hour which is expected to achieve a constant service time of $\frac{1}{2}$ minute by encouraging people to have the exact fare ready. Advise on the conditions under which the campaign would be worthwhile.

(3) Cars arrive from a side road at a junction with a main road, according to a random process at a rate of five per minute. Because of the presence of traffic on the main road a side road vehicle clears the junction every 10 seconds, again according to a random process.

A (a)　What percentage of the time are there no cars waiting in the side road?

(b) How many cars will be waiting in the side road on average?

(c) What is the average waiting time?

B (a) Discuss the considerations you would consider relevant to a decision on whether to install traffic lights at the junction.

7 Car Ownership, Discrete Choices and Travel Demand

This chapter considers some aspects of the problem of forecasting demand. We shall concentrate exclusively on the demand for passenger traffic; the principles of forecasting the demand for freight traffic are similar. Whilst no less important, freight movements are inherently much more complicated and harder to describe and forecast; at the same time good data are scarcer. For these reasons the prediction of freight traffic is far less well developed than that of passenger traffic (for discussions of current practice in the UK for road freight see the Advisory Committee on Trunk Road Assessment 1979b and the Committee of Enquiry into Operator's Licensing 1979).

We start with the prediction of private car traffic, because it is now by far the most common means of personal motorized transport in most developed countries. In Great Britain it provided 82% out of a total of 300 thousand million passenger miles in 1978. Consumers' expenditure on purchase and running of private cars was £9327 million as against £1105 million for buses and £763 million for railways. If expenditure by central and local government on construction and maintenance of roads is added, a total of £10,664 million results (British Road Federation 1979). (Consumers' expenditure on transport was 13% of total consumers' expenditure.) Apart from taxi services it is the only surface mode which is growing. In 1977 car ownership per person in Great Britain was about 0.26 and this is officially forecast to grow to something between 0.38 and 0.46 by 2005 (Giles and Worsley 1979).

Groups that have an obvious interest in forecasting developments in car ownership and use are the manufacturers, traders and providers of ancillary services. Because central and local governments have to construct and maintain roads they too have an interest: both economic appraisal and structural design are heavily dependent on traffic levels expected to use the roads in the future. Government has to take the long term view. In the UK there is currently a design, public participation and construction period of 7 to 15 years between inception of a new trunk road and its opening. It is current practice to design such a road on the basis of the traffic it is expected to carry 15 years after opening, and the economic assessment involves traffic flows throughout an assumed 30 year life (see Advisory Committee on Trunk Road Assessment 1977). The Department of Transport is thus faced with the situation of making decisions on expensive and irreversible investments which should, in principle, be highly sensitive to forecasts of a rapidly growing variable up to 45 years into the future. The attraction of forecasting techniques which succeed in producing usable results over this kind of period and which give the appearance of being unresponsive to year to year changes in the expectations of such relevant variables as future real incomes and fuel prices is manifest. We begin by outlining the methods that have been the basis for official forecasting in the UK until relatively recently. We then mention an alternative approach which has had some influence more recently. Fuller accounts of these will be found in Tanner (1978, 1979), Bates, Gunn and Roberts (1978), Giles and Worsley (1979) and Advisory Committee on Trunk Road Assessment (1977, 1979b).

Possibly because of the especially long term nature of official requirements the techniques used have been rather independent of the more 'conventional' models for the demand for durable goods developed by economists. These are summarized next. The material here is treated at greater length in chapter 13 of the excellent text by Deaton and Muellbauer (1980).

Finally, we briefly consider recent developments in what has become known as behavioural demand modelling of travel demand in general; a fundamental text here is Domencich and McFadden (1975) although an enormous literature has developed since then (see, for example, Hensher and Stopher 1979). We do not mention the more 'conventional' techniques such as gravity models, intervening opportunity models, direct demand and abstract mode models, since to do so would be to duplicate many texts; examples are Stopher and Meyburg (1975), Quandt (1970), Jones (1977) and Stubbs, Tyson and Dalvi (1980). Domencich and McFadden (1975) give a brief summary and critique of these techniques in their first two chapters.

By chance there is one mathematical functional form which is common to the material of this chapter and provides a link. It is known as the *logistic function* and we begin with a description of it.

7.1 The logistic function

One of the simplest possible differential equations is

$$\frac{dy(t)}{dt} = \lambda y(t) \tag{7.1}$$

where λ is a constant and t may be interpreted as time (compare (6.5) above). It says that at any time t the rate of change of the variable $y(t)$ is proportional to the current value of the variable. Another way of writing it is as

$$\frac{1}{y(t)} \frac{dy(t)}{dt} = \lambda$$

or

$$\frac{d \log y(t)}{dt} = \lambda \tag{7.2}$$

implying that the *proportionate* rate of change of the variable is constant. The solution is

$$y(t) = y(0) e^{\lambda t} \tag{7.3}$$

where $y(0)$ is the value of $y(t)$ at an initial instant, $t = 0$.

In the case that $\lambda < 0$, $y(t)$ will tend smoothly towards zero, in which case the process is one of exponential, or 'radioactive' decay. Otherwise, when $\lambda > 0$, we have explosive, exponential growth. Equation (7.1) has been used to describe many phenomena such as simple physical depreciation of equipment, compound growth of interest bearing principal and growth in national income. It has also been used to represent the unrestricted growth of a population of organisms (in which case λ is the birth rate) or the number of individuals who currently suffer from an epidemic disease (in which case λ is the contact rate). Such processes are sometimes said to be autocatalytic, because the result of the process itself speeds the process up (see Lotka 1925).

Whilst having the advantage of simplicity, (7.1) is inadequate to describe some situations because the environment cannot sustain a limitless growth. There is assumed to be an absolute maximum or saturation value s. Equation (7.1) may then be replaced by

$$\frac{dy(t)}{dt} = \beta y(t) [s - y(t)] \tag{7.4}$$

In the early stages, when $y(t)$ is small, (7.4) grows like (7.1), with λ approximately equal to βs. In the late stages, as $y(t)$ approaches saturation, the rate of change of $y(t)$ drops towards zero again. A plot of $y(t)$ against t shows an 'S shaped' or sigmoid curve, symmetrical about the half-way point which is defined by $y(t_0) = s/2$. This is a more satisfactory representation of, for example the simple epidemic, where s would be the total population at risk. At any point in time there are $y(t)$ infectives and $[s - y(t)]$ remaining to be infected. If the two sub-populations mix homogeneously then the number of new cases in unit time will be proportional to the product of these two terms, as in (7.4).

The solution to (7.4) is the *logistic function*

$$y(t) = \frac{s}{1 + k\,e^{-\beta st}} \tag{7.5}$$

where k is a constant such that

$$\log k = \beta s t_0 \tag{7.6}$$

Bailey (1957) shows how a simple extension of (7.4) to allow for removal of infectives due to isolation, recovery or death yields a useful model of some epidemic processes. Lotka

(1925) was an early writer to use a similar model to describe the relationships between populations of predators and of their prey which has recently found application in the economics of fisheries (V. L. Smith 1972) and Marxian conflict between owners of capital and labour (Goodwin 1967).

The analogy between the spread of disease and the spread of information through a population has been exploited by several authors, notably Griliches (1957) and Mansfield (1968), to model the diffusion of technical innovations through populations of manufacturers. Others have used it to analyse the adoption of new products, brands and models of consumer goods.

7.2 The application to car ownership forecasting

The history of the development of the techniques for national car ownership forecasting at the UK Transport and Road Research Laboratory, which came to be adopted for official purposes, is related by Tanner (1978). The logistic function (7.5) was used at an early stage, with $y(t)$ representing car ownership per head of population, β regarded as a constant to be estimated from aggregate time series data and the saturation level fixed by appeal to various arguments at 0.4 cars per person. This was done without any explicit mention of the ideas of diffusion of new products mentioned in the previous section, but rather because the function could be made to fit the data then available as well as the alternatives and is bounded above by a saturation value: a requirement that was, and is still, regarded as axiomatic in some quarters.

In the early 1970s it was decided that the method then in use was unsatisfactory in that both the interpretation of past growth and forecasts of future growth were entirely independent of movements in real personal incomes and motoring costs. The response was to maintain the logistic function (7.5) but to allow the parameter which determines the growth rate of ownership, β, to vary according to

$$\beta = a + b \frac{1}{i} \frac{di}{dt} + c \frac{1}{p} \frac{dp}{dt} \qquad (7.7)$$

In (7.7) a, b and c are constants to be estimated; b is the coefficient of the proportionate rate of change of i, real gross domestic product *per capita* (as a measure of income) and c is the coefficient of the proportionate rate of change of p, an index of real motoring costs.

The solution of (7.5), when β is given by (7.7), is

$$y(t) = \frac{s}{1 + ki^{-bs}p^{-cs}e^{-ast}} \tag{7.8}$$

and at any point in time the elasticity of car ownership with respect to income is $b[s - y(t)]$ and that with respect to motoring costs is $c[s - y(t)]$.

At the time of adopting (7.8) the estimate of saturation was revised to 0.45 cars per person on the grounds discussed at length in Tanner (1978). It was also necessary to obtain values for b and c. These were estimated from Family Expenditure Survey data, international comparisons and regional analysis. Values of b ranged from 3 to 7 giving an income elasticity of 1.0 at the central value of 5, with the 1975 level of car ownership of 0.25 cars per person.

Values of c ranged from -1 to -4, giving a price elasticity of 0.4 at a value of -2.

Given assumed values for the constants s, b and c the constant a was estimated by transforming (7.8) to

$$\log\left(\frac{y(t)}{s - y(t)}\right) - bs\log i - cs\log p = ast - \log k \tag{7.9}$$

Ordinary least squares regression of the variable on the left-hand side of (7.9) on t provided an estimate of as and hence a. The transform of (7.8) represented by (7.9) is a common and simple one to allow the use of linear regression analysis to estimate the parameter β of the logistic, *providing* that a prior value of saturation is available; but it has some drawbacks as we shall see.

Given these estimates of the actual growth in car ownership from 1952 to 1972, about 45% was attributed to increasing real incomes, 15% to decreasing real motoring costs and 40% to the 'pure' time effect represented by the constant a. This illustrates the extent to which the modification to the simple logistic succeeds in introducing economic factors to the explanation of growth in car ownership. However, there are limitations. First, the estimates of b and c were very uncertain as we have seen — for instance the estimates of c varied by a factor of four which means that the implied price elasticity also varies by a factor of four. Different values imply different weights in the explanation to be given to the economic factors. More importantly, the long run future values of car ownership are dominated by the saturation value chosen and this was assumed not to vary with expected future incomes or motoring costs. Changes in these will certainly cause changes in the short and medium term values of predicted car ownership, but in the long run it gets close to saturation whatever happens to them.

As we have already argued, what is forecast to happen in the long term is important in the applications for which the forecasts are intended. The Advisory Committee on Trunk Road Assessment (1977) carried out tests of the sensitivity of the estimated economic rates of return on a selection of 25 current trunk road schemes and showed them to be more sensitive to variations in the saturation value chosen for the traffic forecasts than to any other factor save the rate of discount. This is not surprising since the return from building a road must depend heavily on the amount of traffic expected to use it over the whole of its life. It is unfortunate, then, that the evidence on what the saturation value should be is so inconclusive. A large number of approaches have been used in the attempt to determine it and a wide range of evidence has been used. The estimates range from 0.34 to 0.66 cars per head. Further, very little evidence has been cited to justify the assumption that ultimate saturation will be independent of the levels of personal incomes or the eventual costs of motoring.

It is intuitively clear that a degree of uncertainty about saturation is inherent in the approach. Even if it were known with certainty that the logistic is the 'true' underlying specification and if there were no complications caused by changing economic circumstances, the substantial disturbances which occur in the observed data for all manner of reasons make it difficult to judge the slope and ultimate saturation of the curve when the growth process has yet to pass the half-way point. To this uncertainty must be added doubt about the correct functional specification and about the extent to which future economic fortunes will effect the saturation level. These are two components of the uncertainty which are sometimes forgotten or underestimated.

Before turning to an alternative approach we mention a recent development of the logistic technique; Tanner (1978) gives a more detailed summary of this. It became apparent that the relationship between the percentage rate of growth of car ownership and the level of car ownership is not linear, as it would be if (7.8) were a correct specification and if income and motoring costs changed at constant percentage rates. The growth curve is therefore not symmetrical as the logistic would imply, but would reach half of the saturation level over a shorter time period than it takes to achieve the equivalent growth after that. The data were insufficient to differentiate between the various possible functional forms which might represent this and so a generalization of the logistic was used which has one more parameter, n. The 'power growth' model which generalizes (7.8) is

$$y(t) = \frac{s}{1 + (k^{1/n} + at + b \log i + c \log p)^{-n}} \qquad (7.10)$$

and the logistic is a limiting case as $n \to \infty$.

The methods used to estimate the parameters were similar to those already described, although the values adopted for saturation and income elasticity were different; saturation was set at 0.5 cars per person with 0.4–0.6 representing a 'likely range of uncertainty' and the income elasticity was lowered to 0.6 at an ownership of 0.23.

The comparison of the forecasts from the power growth model with the earlier logistic (Tanner 1978) illustrate further the overriding importance of the saturation level chosen for the long run forecasts, although changing the model form and assumptions about income and price elasticities do have some influence in the shorter run. The uncertainty associated with the choice of saturation levels therefore remains, as does the property that saturation is assumed to be independent of alternative views on the long run values of the economic variables.

7.3 Individual household based models

We now turn to an alternative application of logistic-like functions to the problem of predicting car ownership. The approach here is to attempt to identify the factors which determine whether an individual household will own no cars, one car or more cars. If successful the method should be more easily able to identify and forecast the effects of such phenomena as changing household size and composition, changing distribution of incomes amongst households, changing urbanization, changing public transport provision and the acquisition of second cars by households. The school which has developed this line of thought has, in the UK, been working more or less simultaneously with but rather independently of the aggregate approach of the previous section. One of the earliest published contributions was Wooton and Pick (1967) and very comprehensive recent treatments are given by Bates, Gunn and Roberts (1978) and Martin and Voorhees Associates (1980).

An important source of data is cross section survey data. In the case of Bates, Gunn and Roberts' (1978) work the major source was the annual UK Family Expenditure Survey. For any one year this gives estimates of the proportion of households in each of about 15 income groupings who own at least one car. If these proportions are plotted against income a very strong and regular relationship is apparent (Bates, Gunn and Roberts 1978, figure 5). At low incomes there is a steep rise in ownership as income increases. At high incomes the relationship flattens as almost all households own cars. There is a theoretical maximum of 1.0 of course, but crude plots suggest a 'saturation' level slightly less than that. This suggests that household income is a dominant factor in determining the proportion of households which own cars and that the relationship could be represented by a logistic curve. In fact, Bates' work shows that a slightly different function fits the data better. If p_{1+} is the probability that a household will own at least one car and I is household income, the fitted relationship is of the form

$$p_{1+} = \frac{s_1}{1 + e^{-a_1} I^{-b_1}} \tag{7.11}$$

where a_1 and b_1 are constants and s_1 is a saturation value.

This may be compared with the simple logistic (7.5). The difference is that in (7.5) the independent variable t appears as a term in an exponential, whereas in (7.11) the independent variable I is raised to a power. In fact (7.11) is a special case of the 'power growth' function, (7.10), used by Tanner in his development of the aggregate logistic model, as may be seen by setting $k = b = c = 0$, $n = b$, and $a = \exp(a_1/b_1)$. Thus (7.11) shows the same initial rapid response to low values of the independent variable, with a more gentle movement towards saturation at high values.

Having pointed out the similarities between the functional forms used in the aggregate and disaggregate approaches it is important to be aware of the differences. In the former the unit of analyses is the 'average' individual without reference to his particular characteristics or family circumstances, whereas in the latter it is the household. In the former the principal independent variable is time, whereas in the latter it is income. In the disaggregate case there is less difficulty about identifying a value for saturation because the data contain observations representing almost the full range of possibilities, from the very poor households to the very rich, almost completely saturated households. This makes it feasible to estimate the saturation value from the same data as the other parameters — rather than using external evidence as Tanner did. This has the major advantages of internal consistency and providing a soundly based statistical measure of the accuracy with which the value can be estimated from the data. Thus Bates, Gunn and Roberts (1978) were able to estimate s_1 at 0.948 with a standard error of 0.007, suggesting that about 5% of households will choose not to own a car however high their incomes.

There was also a major difference in the statistical technique used to obtain estimates of the parameters. In order to apply a transformation so as to be able to apply linear regression as in (7.9) it is necessary to have a prior estimate of the saturation value. Even if this is available, the technique is liable to give biased estimates of the parameters with unreliable estimates of their standard errors. This is because undue weight is given to the extreme observations and because the constant variance of errors assumed in simple regression is not satisfied. Bates, Gunn and Roberts (1978) illustrate this problem and Domencich and McFadden (1975) discuss it at length and suggest solutions to it. Fortunately the alternative technique of maximum likelihood is available. This allows simultaneous estimation of saturation with the other parameters and also produces a solution which is asymptotically unbiased (i.e. unbiased in large samples) and has the least possible variance of any estimator constructed from the same data. Although maximum likelihood estimates are more expensive to compute than regression estimates the dramatic fall in computing costs over the last few years has made them feasible, and their use is becoming more common (see Domencich and McFadden 1975).

Having fitted (7.11) for one year Bates, Gunn and Roberts (1978) repeated the exercise for a total of seven years (1969–75). Values estimated for b_1 remained relatively stable but those for a_1 became systematically more negative. This was clearly due to the fact that income was being measured at current prices: effectively the units of measurement of I were changing with inflation, requiring a compensating change in the coefficient of I^{-b_1}. Another weakness of the simple specification was that over time there had been a substantial increase in the costs of purchasing and running cars. A solution to both problems was to deflate income by dividing by a suitable index of general prices and to include a deflated motoring cost index term analogous with the income term. Investigation revealed that the effects of increases in motoring costs were in the opposite direction to increases in income but not of a statistically significantly different proportionate magnitude. On these grounds income was deflated directly by an index of motoring costs, thus saving the need to estimate one more parameter. The resulting independent variable was referred to as 'car purchasing income'.

After this adjustment the estimated relationship showed quite remarkable ability to reproduce the time series and cross section variations in household car ownership.

It was acknowledged that the failure to identify a separate relative price effect might well have been due to the unfortunate fact that over the period of estimation the general retail price index and the car price index had moved in a very similar fashion, so that real car prices had hardly varied at all. This has since ceased to be the case and the UK Department of Transport (1980b) has since attempted to identify separate effects.

Having estimated the p_{1+} relationship the next step was to estimate the probability that a household will own two or more cars, given that it owns at least one car, $p_{2+/1+}$. A pure logistic function was found to give a good fit in this case:

$$p_{2+/1+} = \frac{s_2}{1 + \exp(-a_2 - b_2 I)} \tag{7.12}$$

where again, I represents car purchasing income. The saturation value s_2 was estimated at 0.6.

In order to forecast with (7.11) and (7.12) it is necessary to predict future numbers of households in each income group. This was done by assuming that the current income distribution is described by a gamma distribution, the shape of which will remain unchanged in the future. All that is then required is to predict mean household income.

In a final stage the model developed thus far was refitted to the data from about 44,000 household interviews carried out in 1976 in various parts of the country specifically for the Regional Highway Traffic Model (see Martin and Voorhees Associates 1980 and Advisory Committee on Trunk Road Assessment 1979b). Six different kinds of area were distinguished on the basis of a measure of accessibility, defined as the sum of employment in all zones within an hour's travel time weighted by a negative-exponential deterrence function. The models (7.11) and (7.12) were then fitted in each of the six area types to allow, in a crude way, for the influence of factors other than those modelled explicitly. For instance it is well known that ownership is lower than would be predicted on the basis of incomes alone in densely populated urban areas such as London. The model was then to be used to predict changes in local car ownership in each of 3613 zones in the country, in response to predictions of changes in local incomes.

The central difference between the aggregate national forecasts produced by the methods of the previous section and those of the present section is not that the latter attempts to model the behaviour of the individual household. It is also wrong to characterize the disaggregate approach as relying exclusively on cross section data and the aggregate approach as relying on time series data, as some people have done; both methods rely heavily on both techniques. It is rather in the interpretation of the influence of income on ownership. The authors of the household based approach feel that they have found strong evidence from their cross sectional studies that the overwhelming explanation of ownership growth is current income growth, whilst those of the aggregate approach have chosen to attribute about half the growth to the passage of time — or rather to 'growth continuing through time as a result of changes not explicitly identified' (Tanner 1979, p. 17). Tanner has illustrated how his 'power growth' model may be adapted to produce an aggregate time-series analogue of the disaggregate model which has no time trend and similar properties in respect of its response to assumed income growth.

The implication of attributing all growth to income is that the estimates of income elasticities have to bear a much heavier burden, and, of course, the forecasts are much more sensitive to alternative views of the future growth in real incomes. This is shown starkly if incomes are assumed to stop growing entirely. The aggregate approach would still predict an eventual growth to about double current ownership levels, whereas the disaggregate model would predict a complete halt to growth (neglecting the influence of any assumed changes in motoring costs). If the current period of stagnant real incomes is sustained for a reasonably long period then it should become much easier to discriminate between the two approaches. (For the UK Department of Transport's temporary resolution of the conflict between the two approaches see the Department of Transport 1980b.) However, it would be a mistake to underestimate the difficulties in doing this caused by such things as significant errors in the data, the choice of an appropriate measure of income, and uncharted developments in company car ownership stimulated by changes in tax structures and in government constraints on wages and salaries.

7.4 Durables

In concentrating on two approaches to modelling the demand side of car ownership there are many important issues we have neglected. There is the problem of predicting use, as distinct from ownership of cars; this has received less attention than it deserves. Giles and Worsley (1979) give a brief summary of official practice. The supply side has been neglected. This is in fact both important and very complicated because of the longevity of any 'cohort' of new purchases, a highly developed second hand market, non homogeneity of the durable involved and the variability of scrappage rates and ages in response to variations in maintenance costs and purchase prices of old vehicles. Moggridge (1981) is one of the few authors to have tackled this problem. On the demand side consumers' expectations of the future, lags in adjustment to changing circumstances and hysteresis effects may be significant. Some of these have been considered in the 'conventional' economics literature and we now briefly turn to this.

We first show how the ownership of a durable in continuously variable quantity S_t at time t, can be modelled in a simplistic way by the methods of the elementary consumer model of chapter 2. Suppose that the relative prices of nondurables are constant so that their quantities purchased in period t may be represented by the single variable x_t with price p_t. If the consumer's planning horizon ends after T periods his utility may be represented by

$$u(x_1, x_2, \ldots, x_T, S_1, \ldots, S_T) \tag{7.13}$$

The unit price of a durable is v_t. Suppose that the stock, S_t, of the durable at any one time depreciates physically by a fraction δ during a period, leaving a quantity $(1 - \delta)S_t$. Then if purchases of the durable in period t are denoted by d_t, we have the fundamental *stock-flow* relationship

$$S_t = d_t + (1 - \delta) S_{t-1} \tag{7.14}$$

We now make some further strong assumptions on the circumstances facing the consumer. The durable is divisible and can be freely traded at second hand prices equal to new prices per surviving unit. Consumers can borrow or lend freely at the same fixed rate of interest r providing that his assets (the value of his stock of the durable plus the present value of future incomes) match his liabilities. If A_t are his assets at time t then we must have

$$A_t = (1 + r) A_{t-1} + y_t - p_t q_t - v_t d_t \tag{7.15}$$

where r is the rate of interest and y_t is income. Using (7.14) equation (7.15) may be rewritten as

$$A_t = (1 + r) A_{t-1} + y_t - p_t q_t + v_t [S_t - (1 - \delta) S_{t-1}] \tag{7.16}$$

and by recursive substitution this implies the 'lifetime' constraint,

$$\sum_{t=1}^{T} \rho_t p_t q_t + \sum_{t=1}^{T} (\rho_t v_t^*) S_t + \rho_T A_T = W_1 \tag{7.17}$$

Here

$$\rho_t = \frac{1}{(1+r)^{t-1}}$$

is the discount factor which converts a sum of money at one point in time into an equivalent sum t periods earlier at the rate of interest r (compare section 8.1). W_1 is the present value of wealth defined over the life cycle

$$W_1 = v_1 (1 - \delta) S_0 + (1 + r) A_0 + \sum_{t=0}^{T} \rho_t y_t \tag{7.18}$$

that is, the present value of future incomes, plus initial assets, plus the market value of inherited stocks of the durable, plus money inheritances (measured at the end of the initial period. v_t^* is defined by

$$v_t^* = v_t - \frac{v_{t+1}(1-\delta)}{1+r} \qquad (7.19)$$

and is the *rental equivalent price*, or user cost, of holding one unit of the durable for one period. This includes elements of capital gain or loss, physical depreciation and an interest charge on the principal which is 'tied up' in the unit of the durable.

If future prices, interest rates, depreciation rates and incomes were known then the maximization of the utility function (7.13) subject to the constraint (7.17) would be directly analogous to the 'timeless' consumer problem analysed in chapter 2. A demand curve for the durable could be derived. The model clearly involves too many idealized assumptions for it to be of much practical use; Deaton and Muellbauer (1980) discuss the difficulties. The point of introducing it is to introduce the important concept of user cost (7.19) and with it the argument that any satisfactory description of choice behaviour in purchasing durables will need to take account of such things as expectations about future prices and incomes. Note also the central roles played by the rates of depreciation and interest. These are all features which have been somewhat neglected in the approaches to car ownership modelling described in earlier sections.

A simple application of these ideas has been found in the stock adjustment models of the demand for durables. Equation (7.14) may be rewritten as

$$d_t = (S_t - S_{t-1}) + \delta S_{t-1} \qquad (7.20)$$

The stock adjustment model assumes that at each period there is a desired stock S_t^* and that the actual change in stock achieved is some constant proportion of the change required to bring the stock to the required level: $S_t - S_{t-1} = k(S_t^* - S_{t-1})$. We then have

$$d_t = k(S_t^* - S_{t-1}) + \delta S_{t-1} \qquad (7.21)$$

We now require a theory of what determines the desired stock. For instance, we might suppose that there is a simple linear relationship with real disposable income:

$$S_t^* = \alpha + \beta \frac{y_t}{p_t} \tag{7.22}$$

Very often data on current net purchases are more readily available, or of better quality than that on stocks. This may be exploited by means of the Koyck transformation (see, for example, Wallis 1972): by lagging (7.20), substituting in (7.21), using (7.22) and rearranging we get

$$d_t = k\alpha\delta + k\beta \frac{y_t}{p_t} - k\beta(1 - \delta)\frac{y_{t-1}}{p_{t-1}} + (1 - k)d_{t-1}$$

$$\tag{7.23}$$

Deaton and Muellbauer (1980) report estimates of the parameters of (7.23) on British data from 1954 to 1975 which would imply a value for the adjustment coefficient k of 0.8 and a depreciation rate δ of 0.22. They point out, however, that there are statistical reasons for doubting these results and that this simple model is not very adequate. For example, it may not be reasonable to assume that k is independent of economic variables and no explicit account is taken of the issues raised by the user cost concept of (7.19).

An alternative approach is the discretionary replacement model developed in the USA by R. P. Smith (1974, 1975) and Westin (1975). This recognizes that for a long lived and indivisible durable such as a car the majority of purchases are in fact replacement decisions. If R_t is actual replacement demand and R_t^* is normal replacement demand we may write either (following Smith)

$$R_t = k_t R_t^*$$

or (following Westin)

$$R_t = k_t + R_t^* \tag{7.24}$$

where k_t represents deviations owing to current and expected economic conditions and can be made a function of such variables as real disposable incomes, relative prices, consumer confidence and proxies for expectations such as unemployment rates. R_t^* may be determined *a priori* from information about the age distribution of the car stock (Smith) or it may be estimated statistically (Westin). To (7.24) is added a term to represent new demand that depends on the current levels of some of the variables in k_t (rather after the Bates model of section 7.3) and on historical purchasing patterns to allow for the effects of variations in the proportions of cars of different ages on such things as scrapping rates (an important phenomenon discussed in detail by Moggridge 1981).

The results of Weston's model are compared with those of a stock adjustment model by Deaton and Muellbauer (1980) who argue that the discretionary replacement model provides a more plausible formulation. They note, incidentally, that whilst the models have similar long run responses to price and income changes, the discretionary replacement version exhibits much higher short run effects.

The household based model of section 7.2 explicitly recognized that the car is a non-divisible item and a household faces a discrete choice between owning no cars, one or more cars. The economics literature that we have summarized so far in this section regards the durable as a divisible item, although it does have the advantage that it puts the choice problem in an explicit utility maximizing framework. Indivisibilities may be introduced in a simple way as follows.

Suppose that the annual net cost of car ownership is v^* (as in (7.19)). If annual expenditure is m then the budget constraint is

$$px + v^*S - m \qquad (7.25)$$

where p and x are price and quantity of other goods and $S = 1$ if a car is owned and $S = 0$ if not. Write utility as

$$u(x, S, \epsilon)$$

where ϵ is a parameter to represent variations between households in tastes and family composition. The two possible ownership levels are then

$$u\left(\frac{m}{p}, 0, \epsilon\right) \quad \text{or} \quad u\left(\frac{m - v^*}{p}, 1, \epsilon\right) \qquad (7.26)$$

Households will decide to own a car if the latter exceeds the former. For a given type of household (i.e. for a given ϵ) this defines a threshold level m of income at which income is just sufficient to induce ownership. If $f(m, \epsilon)$ is the joint density function of incomes and household types then the proportion of owning households will be

$$\int_0^\infty \int_{-\infty}^{\phi(m/v^*)} f(m, \epsilon)\, d\epsilon\, dx \qquad (7.27)$$

where $\phi(m/v^*)$ is an increasing function of x/v^* and is the highest level of ϵ that results in ownership. As average income increases, or the durable price falls, the proportion of owners will follow a sigmoid curve.

We have, in effect, derived the model described in section 7.3 from a basic utility maximizing framework. Note the analogy between m/v^* here and the notion of 'car purchasing income'.

Some of the most recent developments in car ownership modelling have concerned the modelling of such phenomena as habit formation and lagged responses to changes. Deaton and Muellbauer (1980) give a brief summary of the durables literature and Moggridge (1981) surveys some of the problems in the car ownership context. Tanner (1979) has given an instructive illustration of how lagged response to income growth might be incorporated in his 'power growth' model of (7.10). He suggests replacing the simple linear term in time, at, by $ag(t)$, where,

$$g(t) = w(t) - w(0)$$

and

$$w(t) = \int_{n=-\infty}^t \exp[-\lambda(t-u)]\log i(u)\, du \qquad (7.28)$$

Here $w(t)$ is an exponentially declining weighted average of the logarithm of past incomes. For example, if incomes have grown at the rate of $100\alpha\%$ per year in the past and do not grow at all in the future, then

$$g(t) = \begin{cases} \alpha t/\lambda & -\infty < t < 0 \\ \alpha(1 - e^{-\lambda t})/\lambda^2 & 0 < t < \infty \end{cases} \qquad (7.29)$$

This shows that $g(t)$ will grow in the future. Hence car ownership will grow in the future by (7.10), purely as a result of the delayed response to historical income growth. There are many alternative ways in which this kind of effect might be represented. A major difficulty, however, is in obtaining data and devising a suitable statistical technique which would allow one to discriminate between them, as Tanner illustrates.

7.5 Behavioural travel demand models

In the previous section we have mentioned the difficulties posed by the problem of handling the indivisibilities of durable goods purchasing decisions within the framework of traditional consumer theory. Yet many transport decisions facing individuals are inherently indivisible: one either makes a trip or does not, owns a car or no car, travels by car or by bus, to destination A or B. The process of the aggregate demand for something changing because all consumers of it slightly adjust their demand is fundamentally different from that of a relatively few number of individuals making a relatively large change in their behaviour (for instance making their daily trip to work by car instead of by bus) whilst the majority carry on as before.

This is one reason why economists — notably McFadden — have developed discrete choice theory. This has found application in several fields in addition to transport modelling (McFadden 1976, gives a survey). A second motive was a deep dissatisfaction with the lack of a sound and consistent theory of individual choice underlying the commonly used methods.

Urban transport planning based on conventional transportation models has become a commonplace, influential and very expensive activity. All over the world local authorities and central governments use standard techniques and packaged algorithms to assess the likely impacts of road improvements, traffic management schemes, relocation of housing, workplaces and shopping centres, changes in public transport services and so forth. Although they have proved to be extremely useful they exhibit features which are unsatisfactory. They are essentially descriptive, fitting models with origins in the physical sciences to aggregate traffic flows between aggregate zones. They do not attempt to represent and are not consistent with any theory of rational decision-making by the individual. It is unusual that satisfactory consideration is given to the statistical properties of the estimator and this encourages planners to ignore such problems as bias and forecasting error. Frequently they are not well suited to analysing relevant policy questions and they can be very expensive (Domencich and McFadden 1975, give a brief summary and critique). In contrast, the 'behavioural' approach begins by considering the choice between discrete alternatives facing the individual. This yields a prediction of his probability of choice of particular travel patterns depending upon his socio-economic circumstances and upon the attributes of the various alternatives as he sees them. Given certain clearly stated assumptions on the statistical nature of this choice procedure, estimators with known and desirable properties can be defined. The resulting parameter estimates can then be used to predict the effect of policy and other changes on the probabilities of a sample of different individuals making particular travel decisions and then these can be combined to yield aggregate policy predictions. Thus, for instance, Domencich and McFadden (1975) are able to estimate the influence of the number of preschool children in a household on the housewife's perceived accessibility of various shopping centres and hence the effect, of say, an increase in fares on her shopping frequency. They are also able to estimate the impact of changes in walking, waiting and travelling times on the probabilities that a worker will choose to travel at an off-peak time and by one mode rather than another.

The central features are that: (a) it is founded on hypotheses concerning utility maximizing choice behaviour of individuals; (b) the alternatives are typically discrete and mutually exclusive; (c) there is an explicit theory of how differences between individuals are statistically distributed throughout the population; (d) questionnaire responses of sampled individuals are used directly in the estimation techniques: they are not aggregated into zonal averages, a procedure which is wasteful of information provided by within zone variations in the data; (e) these techniques (typically maximum likelihood) produce explicit estimates of the reliability of the estimates they produce; (f) the assumed restrictions on behaviour which are necessary to reduce the problem to manageable proportions can be related directly to equivalent restrictions on the form of the individual's preferences and utility function; and (g) the economic evaluation of a change in demand caused by, for instance, a fare change can be related to the assumed preference structure.

In what follows we briefly summarize the approach taken in the pioneering work of Domencich and McFadden by way of an example. There are many alternative approaches and many critics of this particular approach and of the technique in general. Williams (1979) gives a useful non-technical survey.

As a preliminary we define the Weibull distribution of a random variable and mention some of its properties. A random variable η_i has a cumulative Weibull distribution if

$$\text{Prob}\,(\eta_i \leqslant \eta) = \exp\,(-e^{-(\eta + \alpha)}) \tag{7.30}$$

This distribution has a single parameter α which is clearly the mode. For $\alpha = 0$ the distribution has a mean of 0.575, a variance of 1.622 and a slight skew. It has an appearance similar to a normal distribution with mean of $\frac{1}{2}$ and unit variance. It is obvious from (7.30) that adding a constant ν to the random variable η_i gives a new random variable with a Weibull distribution and parameter $\alpha_i - \nu$. A second and most important property is that if we take a set of values of random variables, $\{\eta_1, \ldots, \eta_n\}$, each drawn from independent Weibull distributions with parameter α_i, then the maximum value attained in this set of values is itself a random variable with a Weibull distribution having parameter

$$-\log \sum_{i=1}^{n} \exp(-\alpha_i) \tag{7.31}$$

The Weibull is thus stable under maximization, just as the normal is stable under addition (the sum of two normally distributed random variables is itself normally distributed). This makes it a natural distribution to work with in economic problems involving maximization. Finally, it is quite easy to show that if η_1 and η_2 are two independent Weibull distributed random variables and ν_1 and ν_2 are constants then

$$\text{Prob}\,(\nu_1 + \eta_1 \geqslant \nu_2 + \eta_2) = \frac{\exp(\nu_1 - \alpha_1)}{\exp(\nu_1 - \alpha_1) + \exp(\nu_2 - \alpha_2)}$$
(7.32)

(the generalization to several random variables is straightforward). By rewriting (7.32) as

$$\text{Prob}\,(\nu_1 + \eta_1 \geqslant \nu_2 + \eta_2) = \frac{1}{1 + k\,\exp(\nu_2 - \nu_1)} \quad (7.33)$$

where $k = \exp(\alpha_1 - \alpha_2)$, this is seen to be a logistic function, (7.5).

As an example, consider now the problem of choosing between two alternative modes, 1 and 2, for a particular trip. The modes will have different attributes, such as time taken, money costs, comfort and convenience and so on. We list these attributes in a vector x, and denote the values provided by mode 1 by x^1 and the values provided by mode 2 by x^2. Suppose now that the utility enjoyed by a particular individual whose socio-economic characteristics are specified by the vector s is given by

$$U(x, s) = V(x, s) + \eta(x, s) \quad (7.34)$$

where $V(x, s)$ is non-stochastic and reflects the 'representative' tastes of the population and $\eta(x, s)$ is a random variable (with mean independent of s) which reflects the effect of individual idiosyncrasies in tastes or unobserved attributes of the alternatives.

The individual will choose alternative 1 if it yields him a higher level of utility. Therefore if P_1 is the probability that an individual selected at random will select alternative 1:

$$P_1 = \text{Prob}\,[U(x^1, s) > U(x^2, s)]$$
$$= \text{Prob}\,[\eta(x^2, s) - \eta(x^1, s) < V(x^1, s) - V(x^2, s)]$$
(7.35)

But providing that the random components are independent Weibull-distributed, this immediately yields the logistic probability function in (7.33). We now make the further assumption that $V(x, s)$ is linear in its parameters:

$$V(x^j, s) = \beta_1 x_1^j + \beta_2 x_2^j \qquad (7.36)$$

Equation (7.35) then becomes

$$P_1 = \frac{1}{1 + k \exp[\beta_1(x_1^1 - x_1^2) + \beta_2(x_2^1 - x_2^2)]} \qquad (7.37)$$

In (7.37) the exponents are differences in cost and time on the two modes. k is known as the 'mode specific' effect; if k were unity and costs and times were equal on the two modes, then P_1 would be $\frac{1}{2}$, but if k were 2 then P_1 would be 1/3. It thus accounts for any 'bias' in favour of one mode which individuals may display even if there are no measured differences in the attributes of the modes. This is a strict utility model which exhibits the property of the independence of irrelevant alternatives: that the relative probabilities of choosing two alternatives depends only on their relative utilities and not on those of any others. Unless 'alternatives' are carefully defined this may have peculiar implications which are discussed by Domencich and McFadden (1975).

Equation (7.37) may be estimated by standard maximum likelihood techniques (see the previous section) from a suitable sample of individuals who have made choices when faced with the two alternatives which gives information about the attributes of the alternatives, the characteristics of the individuals and their actual decisions.

The derivation of (7.37) provides an elegant rationalization of the use of the logistic in mode choice studies, something which has been done in an *ad hoc* way for many years in conventional transportation studies. It is also very closely related to techniques used to measure the valuation of time implicit in people's behaviour; these began with Beesley (1965) and were developed by Quarmby (1967). In essence this depends upon the observation that if x_1 is time taken and x_2 is money cost, and if the time difference between the two modes were to increase by one minute and the cost difference fall by £β_1/β_2, then modal choice probabilities would be unchanged. Thus by his behaviour the individual is revealing that one minute is equivalent to $£\beta_1/\beta_2$, and so estimates of the parameters in (7.41) provide an estimate of the marginal value of time to him. Bruzelius (1979) gives a good survey of the subject of the value of time.

Since it is desired to model the trip frequency, destination choice, time of day choice and mode choice, work and residential location and vehicle ownership decisions, the structure of possibilities facing the individual would be impossibly complicated to model and estimate without some very strong restrictions on the decision mechanism. Thus the way in which the various attributes of different modes, such as costs and times, influence modal choice might be assumed not to depend upon the time of day chosen, although the attributes themselves will change with the time of day. Then the time of day choice could be considered, assuming that the most advantageous mode will be chosen for each time of day. In this way a decision 'tree' could be constructed and, when considering choices at a point on this tree, the relevant information pertaining to points higher up the tree can be summarized in a single 'inclusive price index'. It is this which reduces the estimation problem to manageable proportions. In some contexts the inclusive price index can be interpreted as a natural and pleasing measure of accessibility — for instance in the housewife's decision about whether and where to shop.

To illustrate how this works suppose that there are two possible modes for a work trip indexed $m = a$ or $m = b$, and two possible times of day, indexed $t = p$ (peak, say) or $t = o$ (off-peak). One could model the choice between the four alternatives as a simultaneous decision by using a generalization of (7.37). But the problem can be simplified and the number of parameters to be estimated can be greatly reduced if we assume that the consumer makes his decision in two stages. We first look at the choice of mode, *given* that a time of day has been selected, and then look at the choice of time of day using information from the previous stage concerning the attributes of the mode that was considered best at each time of day.

Suppose that x^{mt} is a sub-vector of the vector x in (7.34) which contains all those attributes which vary with the time of day only. We split $V(\mathbf{x}, \mathbf{s})$ in (7.34) according to

$$V(\mathbf{x}, \mathbf{s}) = V^1(\mathbf{x}^{mt}, \mathbf{s}) + V^2(\mathbf{x}^t, \mathbf{s})$$
$$= V^1_{mt} + V^2_t \qquad (7.38)$$

That decisions can be split up in this way and utility be written in additively separable form is an important assumption which needs to be tested aginst evidence.

Now let $P_{m|t}$ be the probability of choosing mode m given that time t has been chosen. Then, for instance, the probability of choosing mode a in the peak will be given by

$$P_{a|p} = \text{Prob}\,(V^1_{ap} + \eta_{ap} > V^1_{bp} + \eta_{bp})$$
$$= \frac{\exp(V^1_{ap} - \alpha_{ap})}{\exp(V^1_{ap} - \alpha_{ap}) + \exp(V^1_{bp} - \alpha_{bp})} \qquad (7.39)$$

by analogy with (7.32). Here the α_{mp} are the parameters of the independent Weibull-distributed η_{mp}.

Now consider P_p, which is the probability of choosing the peak time of day when the most appropriate mode has been chosen for each time of day. This will be given by

$$P_p = \text{Prob}\,[V^2_p + \max_{m=a,b}\,(V^1_{mp} + \eta_{mp})$$
$$> V^2_o + \max_{m=a,b}\,(V^1_{mo} + \eta_{mo})] \qquad (7.40)$$

The terms $(V^1_{mt} + \eta_{mt})$ are each Weibull random variables with parameters $\alpha_{mt} - V^1_{mt}$. Hence, by (7.31) the random variable

$$\eta_p = \max_{m=a,b}\,(V^1_{mp} + \eta_{mp})$$

also has a Weibull distribution with parameter

$$y_p = -\log\,[\exp(V^1_{ap} - \alpha_{ap}) + \exp(V^1_{bp} - \alpha_{bp})] \qquad (7.41)$$

Applying the analogy with (7.32) again to (7.40) we have that

$$P_p = \frac{\exp(V^2_p - y_p)}{\exp(V^2_p - y_p) + \exp(V^2_o - y_o)} \qquad (7.42)$$

Equation (7.42) expresses the binary choice probabilities between times of day in terms of the non-stochastic utilities of the different times of day, V_t^2, and an 'index' of the desirability of travel at those times, taking into account the attributes of the alternative modes, y_m. We can now complete the analysis by showing how this index may be obtained from the estimates of the conditional probabilities in (7.39).

Write (7.41) as

$$y_p(q_a, q_b) = -\log[\exp(q_a) + \exp(q_b)] \qquad (7.43)$$

where

$$q_m = (V_{mp}^1 - \alpha_{mp}) \quad m = a, b \qquad (7.44)$$

Let $\bar{q}$ be the average of the q_i:

$$\bar{q} = \tfrac{1}{2}(q_a + q_b)$$

and take the Taylor expansion of (7.43) about the point (q_a, q_b):

$$y_p(\bar{q}, \bar{q}) = y_p(q_a, q_b) + \frac{\partial y_p(q_a, q_b)}{\partial q_a}(\bar{q} - q_a)$$

$$+ \frac{\partial y_p(q_a, q_b)}{\partial q_b}(\bar{q} - q_b) + \text{higher-order terms}$$

$$\qquad (7.45)$$

But

$$\frac{\partial y_p}{\partial q_m} = \frac{-\exp(q_m)}{\exp(q_a) + \exp(q_b)} \quad m = a, b$$

and comparing this with (7.44) and (7.39) we see that

$$\frac{\partial y_p}{\partial q_m} = -P_{m|p} \quad m = a, b$$

Hence from (7.45)

$$y_p(q_a, q_b) = y_p(\bar{q}, \bar{q}) + (P_{a|p} + P_{b|p})\bar{q}$$

$$- (P_{a|p}q_a + P_{b|p}q_b) - \text{higher-order terms}$$

Using (7.43) with $q_a = q_b = \bar{q}$ and the fact that

$$P_{a|p} + P_{b|p} = 1$$

gives

$$y_p(q_a, q_b) = -\log 2 + (\alpha_{ap}P_{a|p} + \alpha_{bp}P_{b|p})$$
$$- (P_{a|p}V_{ap}^1 + P_{b|p}V_{bp}^1) - \text{higher-order terms}$$
$$(7.46)$$

Assuming now a linear form for the V_{mp}^1, as in (7.36),

$$V_{mp}^1 = \sum_{k=1}^{K} \beta_k f^k(x^{mp}, s)$$

where the $f^k(x^{mt}, s)$ are functions of the attributes, x^{mt}, (7.46) becomes

$$y_p = -\sum_{k=1}^{K} \beta_k [P_{a|p}Z^k(x^{ap}, s) + P_{b|p}Z^k(x^{bp}, s)]$$
$$(7.47)$$

(In moving from (7.46) to (7.47) the constants have been absorbed in the β_k, and it is assumed that the higher-order terms may be neglected.) Thus, the inclusive cost of a trip (at a particular time) by the best available mode can be measured by weighting the variables for the alternative modes by the corresponding modal split probabilities and summing over these weighted variables using the coefficients estimated from empirical modal splits at a fixed time.

Now, everything on the right-hand side of (7.47) is known from the estimation of the conditional probability in (7.39). Hence, in the estimation of the time of day probabilities, in (7.42), the single index (7.47) can be calculated and used as a summary of the modal choice problem. When there are many modes, many possible times of day and many separate decision stages, the generalization of the analysis provides a way of simplifying the choice problem sufficiently for it to be tractable and for there to be sufficiently few parameters for them to be estimated from a sample of a reasonable size.

The final two chapters of Domencich and McFadden (1975) report an application of the theory to data pertaining to Pittsburgh. This was not a specially executed survey; use was made of data from a suitable home interview survey of 1967. Despite the relatively small samples the model does appear to perform well, with sensible and, on the whole, highly significant coefficients and a good ability to predict observed decisions within the sample. It would be wrong to regard this as a definitive study of Pittsburgh, and dangerous to assume that the results would necessarily apply to other places because so many of the variables found to be important might differ. However, some of the results are of sufficient potential importance for policy purposes to be worth mentioning. It was found that in this sample of work trips, travellers attach the same weight to a minute spent at a bus stop as they do travelling in either the bus or car, but the disutility of time spent walking to or from a bus stop was three to four times higher. The implicit time values were $1.10 per hour for travelling and $3.94 per hour for walking.

In shopping behaviour the authors were successful in modelling the choice between two modes, the peak–off-peak choice, the choice between three to five destinations and the shopping trip frequency. This amply demonstrates the power of the simplifying assumptions in facilitating the description of a very complex choice structure. The value of travelling time was lower at $0.95 per hour and of walking time higher at $5.46 per hour, reflecting the increased inconvenience of walking when small children and the carrying of shopping are involved. Some surprisingly high elasticities are implied for the typical individual. For instance, the elasticity of the car mode choice with respect to car travelling time is about -1, and that of the off-peak rather than peak is -2. Similarly, the strip frequency elasticity is -1.7. Sample average elasticities are expected to be a half to three-quarters of these values. The implication is that parking charges or fares which differentiate between peak and off-peak travel, or between different areas according to relative congestion would be powerful tools for policy-makers.

In chapter 2 we showed that the 'area under the demand curve' measure of consumer benefit from a price change can be related to fundamental measures of consumer benefit in terms of consumer preference. We complete this chapter by showing (after Domencich and McFadden 1975) that this can still be done when the demand curve is generated by a few individuals changing discrete choices rather than by all individuals changing continuously variable demands.

As in section 2.6 imagine that the price of a trip falls from p^0 to p. Suppose that the relative prices of all other goods remain constant so that we can represent quantities consumed by the composite variable $y(p)$. We assume that the utility function of the individual may be scaled to be linear in $y(p)$:

$$u(y, \mathbf{x}, \mathbf{s}) = y(p) + V(\mathbf{x}, \mathbf{s}) + \eta(\mathbf{x}, \mathbf{s}) \qquad (7.48)$$

which may be compared with (7.34). Suppose that the individual has a choice between a transport alternative with attributes $\mathbf{x}^1$ and a non-transport alternative with attributes $\mathbf{x}^0$.

The consumer will choose the transport alternative at price p if

$$y(p) + V(\mathbf{x}^0, \mathbf{s}) + \eta(\mathbf{x}^0, \mathbf{s}) < y(p)$$
$$-p + V(\mathbf{x}^1, \mathbf{s}) + \eta(\mathbf{x}^1, \mathbf{s}) \qquad (7.49)$$

that is, if

$$\eta(\mathbf{x}^0, \mathbf{s}) - \eta(\mathbf{x}^1, \mathbf{s}) < V(\mathbf{x}^1, \mathbf{s}) - V(\mathbf{x}^0, \mathbf{s}) - p \quad (7.50)$$

If G denotes the cumulative distribution of the differences of the random components in utility in (7.48) then the *per capita* demand for the transport alternative will, from (7.50), be given by

$$D(p) = G[V(\mathbf{x}^1, \mathbf{s}) - V(\mathbf{x}^0, \mathbf{s}) - p] \qquad (7.51)$$

Then the area measure of benefit from a fall from p^0 to p corresponding to (2.35) and to the area $B + D$ in figure 1.2 is

$$\int_p^{p^0} G[V(\mathbf{x}^1, \mathbf{s}) - V(\mathbf{x}^0, \mathbf{s}) - z]\, dz \qquad (7.52)$$

where the curve is taken as being drawn in *per capita* terms. In a cost benefit analysis it would be necessary to subtract from the gross benefit figure the costs of the resources consumed in the implementation of the project. Now, the individual consumer will attain the utility level

$$\max [y(p) + V(\mathbf{x}^0, \mathbf{s}) + \eta(\mathbf{x}^0, \mathbf{s}),$$
$$y(p) - p + V(\mathbf{x}^0, \mathbf{s}) + \eta(\mathbf{x}^1, \mathbf{s})]$$

$$= y(p) + V(x^0, s) + \eta(x^1, s)$$
$$+ \max [\eta, V(x^1, s) - V(x^0, s) - p]$$
(7.53)

where η is the left-hand side of (7.50):

$$\eta = \eta(x^0, s) - \eta(x^1, s)$$

Aggregate welfare *per capita*, W, will be attained by taking the mathematical expectation of this expression over all individuals, the relevant distribution function being given by $G'(\eta)$:

$$W = \text{constant} + y(p)$$

$$+ \int_{-\infty}^{\infty} \max [\eta, V(x^1, s) - V(x^0, s) - p] \, G'(\eta) \, d\eta$$

$$= \text{constant} + y(p) + \lambda G(\lambda) + \int_{\lambda}^{\infty} \eta G'(\eta) \, d\eta \quad (7.54)$$

where λ is the right-hand side of (7.50):

$$\lambda = V(x^1, s) - V(x^0, s) - p$$

Using the assumption that

$$E\eta = \int_{-\infty}^{\infty} \eta G'(\eta) \, d\eta = 0$$

and integrating by parts, (7.54) simplifies to

$$W = \text{constant} + y(p) + \int_{-\infty}^{\lambda} G(\eta) \, d\eta$$

Hence the change in aggregate welfare is

$$\Delta W = y(p^0) - y(p) + \int_{\lambda}^{\lambda^0} G(\eta) \, d\eta$$

$$= y(p^0) - y(p) + \int_{v^1 - v^0 - p}^{v^1 - v^0 - p^0} G(\eta) \, d\eta$$

$$= y(p^0) - y(p) + \int_{p}^{p^0} G(v^1 - v^0 - \eta) \, d\eta \quad (7.55)$$

But the expression in (7.55) for the *per capita* social welfare change is the same as (7.52) for the area under the *per capita* demand function adjusted for any net change in the consumption of other commodities which is necessary in order to cover the resource costs of implementing the fare change.

We have therefore confirmed the validity of using the conventional cost benefit measures of consumer benefit by measuring areas under aggregate demand curves, even if those demand curves are generated by individuals making discrete choices. This is a valuable result in that it provides a formal basis for evaluation techniques used in planning studies which use behavioural demand models. This is a feature which has been lacking in some of the conventional urban transportation models. Like the justification put forward in chapter 2, it does rely heavily on the assumptions made, in particular the assumption embodied in (7.48) that the utility function can be written in a form which is linear in the composite 'other goods'. This is very similar to the restrictions imposed in chapter 2.

8 Economic Evaluation, Investment Criteria and Public Enterprise Objectives

In this chapter we consolidate some of the ideas which were introduced in chapter 5. We first illustrate how choosing the scale of investment in infrastructure according to the criterion of maximizing the net present value of future benefits (that is, using discounted cash flow techniques) will lead to simultaneous short run and long run marginal cost pricing and to the efficient size of enterprise. We then compare the results of using this criterion with those which emerge from such alternatives as monopolistic profit maximization or passenger miles maximization. We discuss the problem of the estimation of the magnitude of the losses in welfare which may be due to the adoption of the 'wrong' criterion and to the failure to take adequate account of the failure of competitive markets. This provides the background for a discussion of government policy towards public enterprises and for the discussion of market intervention and regulation in chapter 9.

8.1 Present value maximization

Suppose that a particular good or service is provided not by a perfectly competitive market but by a large publicly owned or controlled enterprise which has a degree of monopoly power. This situation is perhaps the most common one in modern transport industries although it was much less so in the first three decades of this century and before, when bus, tram and railway services were provided by private companies often in fierce competition. A public enterprise will normally be directed to operate 'in the public interest' and let us sup-

pose that it is agreed that this be interpreted to mean that
pricing and investment rules be set so as to maximize the
present value of the future social benefits net of all costs.
We now illustrate that this will be consistent with the efficiency conditions identified in chapters 4 and 5.

One of the most important problems in investment planning is obviously that of uncertainty about the future. We
wish to abstract from this problem here so as to analyse the
simplest possible case where the future is certain – or rather
the enterprise acts as if there were no uncertainty about it.
We suppose that the demand for the service at any future
time t if price $p(t)$ is charged will be $f(p(t), t)$. There are two
inputs to production: labour must be paid a wage of $w(t)$ and
is a variable input which is used in amount $L(t)$ (the analysis
is easily generalized to include more variable inputs); the
other input is 'capital' or capacity (infrastructure, rolling
stock, etc.) K which is not variable but must be fixed at the
initial planning stage. The cost of a unit of capital is c. The
various amounts of labour may be employed with the capital
to produce output according to the technology specified in
the production relation $F(L(t), K)$. The interest rate (in real
terms) to be used for discounting is r. This may be the cost
of borrowing to the enterprise on the open market or may be
some centrally specified value such as the UK Test Discount
Rate (which in the UK is currently 5% per annum in real
terms on most projects, but 7% for those for which it is
thought that there is a particular risk of project appraisal
optimism).

As in chapter 5 we take the gross benefit at time t to be
given by the willingness to pay, $W(t)$:

$$W(t) = \int_{p(t)}^{\alpha} f(z, t)\, dz + p(t) f(p(t), t) \tag{8.1}$$

As before we have from (8.1) that

$$\frac{dW(t)}{dp(t)} = -f(p(t), t) + p(t) \frac{\partial f(p(t), t)}{\partial p(t)} + f(p(t), t)$$

$$= p(t) \frac{\partial f(p(t), t)}{\partial p(t)} \tag{8.2}$$

The problem we have set the enterprise is to choose the price $p(t)$ to charge in each future period, the amount of labour $L(t)$ to use, and the scale K of the project. The objective is the present value of all future benefit, net of the cost of the initial investment:

$$\sum_{t=1}^{\infty} \left(\frac{W(t) - w(t) L(t)}{(1+r)^t} \right) - cK \tag{8.3}$$

We need to ensure that each period the demand will be satisfied, i.e.

$$f(p(t), t) = F(L(t), K) \quad t = 1, 2, \ldots \tag{8.4}$$

Let the Lagrangian multipliers associated with each of the constraints in (8.4) be denoted $\lambda(t)$. Then forming the Lagrangian with (8.3) and (8.4), differentiating with respect to $p(t)$ and using (8.2) gives

$$\frac{p(t)}{(1+r)^t} = \lambda(t) \tag{8.5}$$

at a maximum. Hence each shadow price is the present value of a unit sale at the respective future period.

Maximizing with respect to labour employed at each period gives

$$w(t) = (1+r)^t \lambda(t) \frac{\partial F(L(t), K)}{\partial L(t)} \tag{8.6}$$

Eliminating $\lambda(t)$ between (8.5) and (8.6):

$$p(t) \frac{\partial F(L(t), K)}{\partial L(t)} = w(t) \quad t = 1, 2, \ldots \tag{8.7}$$

Like (3.11), this says that at each period the cost of employing one more unit of labour must equal the return from doing so. The latter is the marginal product of the extra labour multiplied by the unit price of the output. Condition (8.7) may be rewritten as

$$p(t) = \frac{w(t)}{\partial F(L(t), K)/\partial L(t)} \quad t = 1, 2, \ldots \tag{8.8}$$

and this may be interpreted as saying that price must always equal short run marginal cost. It is short run because the calculation involves variations in one input (labour) holding the other (capital) constant.

Maximizing the Lagrangian with respect to K gives

$$\sum_{t=1}^{\infty} \lambda_t \frac{\partial F(L(t), K)}{\partial K} = c$$

or, using (8.5),

$$\sum_{t} \frac{p(t)}{(1+r)^t} \frac{\partial F(L(t), K)}{\partial K} = c \qquad (8.9)$$

One extra unit of capacity will produce extra output in each future period, the amount being the marginal product of capital. In (8.9) each increment in output is valued at the price of the output to give the marginal value product, and then the discounted present value of these is calculated. The condition says that this must equal the cost of an extra unit of capital.

There is a sense in which (8.9) says that price should equal long run marginal cost. This may be more easily seen in the special case that wage rates are expected to be constant and demand depends only on price. Then the price and labour employed will not depend upon time and (8.9) will reduce to

$$p \frac{\partial F(L, K)}{\partial K} \sum_{t} \frac{1}{(1+r)^t} = c$$

or

$$p = \frac{rc}{\partial F(L, K)/\partial K} \qquad (8.10)$$

The product rc is the interest cost per period of financing the purchase of a unit of capital. Dividing this by the marginal product of capital converts the right-hand side of (8.10) into the cost of producing one more unit of output per period. It is the *long run* marginal cost because as capital K is adjusted to its optimum, so labour must be adjusted to maintain (8.8). All factors are therefore being allowed to vary. Notice that (8.10) and (8.8) together imply that at the optimum long and short run marginal costs should be the same.

Before drawing further inferences from this analysis we mention some of the simplifying assumptions that have been made. First an infinite time horizon has been used; the analysis may easily be adapted to the case of a finite horizon. Second the capital has been assumed not to suffer physical depreciation; this would complicate the analysis somewhat, as would the existence of terminal or scrap values at the end of a finite time horizon. More seriously the question of the timing of investment has not been considered: if the demand is expected to vary over time and if investment is irreversible the problem of timing can become complicated; Nickell (1979) gives a full analysis. Finally it has been assumed that the capital can be varied continuously whereas indivisibly of investment may be a significant problem in some practical situations. For instance, as we mentioned in chapter 5, all or nothing decisions will have to be made on the basis of non-marginal consumer surplus and user benefit calculations.

We have illustrated that in a simple case the method of designing projects by maximizing their discounted net present benefits, yields the pricing and investment decisions which are necessary conditions for economic efficiency. It is important to note that in this process the scale of the project is determined simultaneously with the price to be charged for it. In practice the fares to be charged are often determined by some quite different criterion such as the 'fair', or historically established rate per mile. This is unlikely to lead to economically efficient investment. If the new facility has lower long run marginal costs than the fare fixed then some trips will be unnecessarily deterred and there will be under-investment. On the other hand if a new, high quality service is to be offered at below its true cost then there will be over-investment if the project goes ahead, or possibly a failure to implement it if, in assessing it, the project is realistically costed and it fails to demonstrate its value.

The next point to note is that if prices and output are fixed by net present value maximization, or equivalently, marginal cost pricing, then the rate of profit follows as a direct consequence. In particular, if there are no fixed costs and constant returns to scale then the optimum pricing and investment policy will just yield a zero profit. This is because marginal costs will be the same at all levels of output and hence equal to average unit costs, which in turn are equal to prices. More formally, constant returns means that the production functions is homogeneous of degree one, so by Euler's theorem

$$F(L(t), K) = \frac{\partial F(L(t), K)}{\partial L(t)} L(t) + \frac{\partial F(L(t), K)}{\partial K} K$$

(8.11)

Using (8.7), (8.10) and rearranging:

$$pF(L(t), K) = w(t) L(t) + rcK \tag{8.12}$$

which simply says that revenue equals cost.

If there are diminishing returns to scale a positive profit before fixed costs will be earned and if there are increasing returns a loss must be incurred. In any of these cases an overall loss may be made once any genuinely fixed costs have been accounted for and this forms one of the classical cases in favour of providing a subsidy from general taxation revenues; the activity is desirable from the point of view of economic efficiency but cannot be provided by a commercially viable private enterprise. Once again, in this analysis we have assumed that the factors of production are divisible and continuously variable. At any point in time it is assumed that labour can be varied sufficiently to produce the required output with the given capital. In cases where there are significant indivisibilities one would have to return to an analysis on the lines of that in section 5.2. Either demand will fall between two discrete levels of capacity, in which case price will be set at short run marginal cost, or capacity will be fully used and price will be set so as to adjust demand to it. The decision on whether or not to invest and expand output would then have to be taken on the basis of a cost benefit analysis. Rees (1976) gives a detailed diagrammatic analysis of how this can be done.

Much of the debate about the case for subsidies has not been about the principles just outlined but about the extent to which the costs of enterprises are genuinely fixed. Import-

ant work in this field is by Joy (1973) who argued that
contrary to conventional wisdom, a very large proportion of
the costs of the British railway system are in fact dependent
upon the traffic levels carried. A further argument against
subsidy which has been cogently presented by Pryke (1977),
amongst others, is that it weakens the incentive to entre-
preneurial efficiency which is provided by the pursuit of
profit.

Others have argued that the waste of resources due to the
failure to achieve technological efficiency (not necessarily in
any way because of external subsidy) is far more significant
than losses due to misallocation of resources because of
inefficient pricing (for example, Harberger 1954).

The practical difficulties of present value appraisals of
defining and measuring marginal costs, and more particularly
the administrative problems of enforcing these criteria, are
reflected in recent UK Treasury statements on the subject in
the Nationalised Industry White Papers of 1967 and 1978.
The result has been to move away from the 'purist' prescription we have outlined, by attempting to impose profitability
targets, productivity requirements, financing constraints and
so on, which strictly speaking should not be necessary and
which may well be mutually inconsistent. The position has
been further complicated by the imposition of price and
other controls associated with general government policy (see
chapter 9). Rees (1976) discusses the nature of the conflicts
between these various policies in some detail.

8.2 Corporate objectives

A strategy adopted by the authorities of simply directing a
public enterprise to adopt project appraisal on the lines of
the previous section and marginal cost pricing and acquiescing
fully in the consequences, is a relatively decentralized one.
Hedging such an instruction with qualifications and supplementary objectives makes it less so. This raises the general
question of the implications of specifying alternative corporate
objectives.

As an alternative to the net social benefit criterion of the
previous section, the centre could specify a selling price and

instruct the enterprise to act as a profit maximizing (or loss minimizing) price taker. It is easy to see that the enterprise would then adopt marginal cost pricing so that so long as the price was set 'correctly' the same outcome would be achieved.

This is known as a decentralization result. A set of prices is specified and a rule of behaviour is specified to each enterprise — and to each management unit within the enterprise. If each decision at every level is taken according to this value, using the given prices then the outcome will be consistent with the centre's objectives.

As an alternative decentralization procedure the idea has recently gained some currency that public transport operators might be directed to run their services so as to maximize the total number of passenger miles they sell, subject to an overall subsidy constraint. The attention given to this strategy has mainly been due to its adoption in January 1975 as a corporate objective for London Transport (1975) and to Quarmby (1977). It has also been suggested as a possible objective for the railways and has been discussed by Nash (1978) in the context of management objectives for bus transport.

Suppose that there are three independent services which might be supplied and that the number of passenger miles per annum demanded at each of the fare levels p_1, p_2 and p_3 pence per passenger mile are given by $f_1(p_1), f_2(p_2)$ and $f_3(p_3)$. These might be alternative modes or alternative services provided by the same mode, such as peak, off-peak and weekend bus services. The following analysis can be generalized in an obvious way to handle any number of services, so this restriction of the analysis is unimportant.

As in chapter 5, suppose that α_i are values such that any fare higher than this will eliminate demand, i.e.

$$p_i \geqslant \alpha_i \Rightarrow f_i(p_i) = 0 \quad i = 1, 2, 3 \qquad (8.13)$$

Assume that the demand relationships have the usual property:

$$\frac{\mathrm{d}f_i(p_i)}{\mathrm{d}p_i} = f_i' < 0 \quad i = 1, 2, 3 \qquad (8.14)$$

Costs, related to service levels, are given by

$$C_i(f_i(p_i))$$

with

$$\frac{dC_i}{df_i} = C_i' > 0 \quad \text{and} \quad C_i'' \geqslant 0 \quad i = 1, 2, 3 \qquad (8.15)$$

The Transport (London) Act 1969 specified London Transport's objective as 'to provide or secure the provision of such public passenger transport services as best meet the needs for the time being of Greater London'. London Transport's interpretation of this, to provide a corporate 'Aim' may be formalized as the following problem:

maximize $f_1(p_1) + f_2(p_2) + f_3(p_3)$

subject to $\Sigma \left[p_i f_i(p_i) - C_i(f_i(p_i)) \right] \geqslant \Pi$ $\qquad (8.16)$

and $\quad 0 \leqslant p_1 \leqslant \alpha_1, 0 \leqslant p_2 \leqslant \alpha_2, 0 \leqslant p_3 \leqslant \alpha_3$

where Π is the contribution towards fixed costs required from net operating revenues. Because of the lump sum subsidy provided this may be either positive or negative.

The necessary conditions for this maximization with respect to the p_i are

$$f_i' + \lambda \left[(p_i - C_i') f_i' + f_i \right] - \delta_i = 0 \quad i = 1, 2, 3 \ (8.17)$$

where $\lambda \geqslant 0$ and $\delta \geqslant 0$ are the Kuhn–Tucker multipliers (or shadow prices) corresponding to the constraints on profit and on fares respectively. We can safely assume that the profit constraint will be binding, hence $\lambda > 0$.

For the sake of the argument let us assume that at the optimum services 1 and 2 are provided, but that service 3 is not; so $\delta_1 = \delta_2 = 0$ and $\delta_3 > 0$ with $p_3 = \alpha_3$. We then have from (8.17)

$$f_1' + \lambda \left[(p_1 - C_1') f_1' + f_1 \right] = 0$$
$$f_2' + \lambda \left[(p_2 - C_2') f_2' + f_2 \right] = 0 \qquad (8.18)$$
$$f_3' + \lambda \left[(p_3 - C_3') f_3' + f_3 \right] > 0$$

In each case the term in square brackets is the marginal net revenue with respect to *price*, call it MR_i, and so the first two equations of (8.18) imply that

$$\frac{MR_1}{MR_2} = \frac{f_1'}{f_2'} \tag{8.19}$$

i.e. that the ratio of the net marginal revenues should equal the ratio of the slopes of the demand curves. Rewriting (8.18) gives

$$p_i - C_i' = -\frac{1}{\lambda}\frac{f_i}{f_i'} = -\frac{1}{\lambda} - \frac{p_i}{\eta_i} \quad i = 1, 2$$

$$\alpha_3 - C_3'(\alpha_3) < -\frac{1}{\lambda} - \frac{f_3(\alpha_3)}{f_3'} \tag{8.20}$$

Relations (8.20) together with the profit constraint determine the optimum fares and service levels, on the assumption that it is optimum not to offer service 3 at all. The parameter λ is the shadow price of the profit constraint and its value measures the extra passenger miles which could be provided at the optimum if £1 extra subsidy were provided. It has the dimensions of passenger miles per pound and corresponds to the 'passmark' used in making decisions about the introduction or expansion of services. Rewriting the third relation of (8.20), remembering that $f_3(\alpha_3) = 0$, gives

$$C_3' - \alpha_3 > 1/\lambda \tag{8.21}$$

which implies that a service will not be provided if the net cost to the system of the first unit (and hence on our assumptions all other units) exceeds the inverse of the system passmark, in pounds per passenger mile. Services which are provided will be provided to the point where

$$C_i' - p_i \left(1 + \frac{1}{\eta_i}\right) = \frac{1}{\lambda} \quad i = 1, 2 \tag{8.22}$$

that is, where marginal cost net of marginal revenue generated is just equal to the inverse pass-mark. Thus, once the pass-mark λ has been established for the whole system a decision to adjust a fare on any individual service can be made at a relatively junior managerial level by comparing the marginal costs and revenues and making changes until (8.22) is satisfied. Similarly decisions to invest or disinvest so as to provide new services, or close old ones, can be made on the basis of (8.21) provided the change is small relative to the whole system. Larger changes would involve a recalculation of the pass-mark.

Referring back to section 5.2 we see that the conditions analogous to (8.20) for the case of an objective of attaining economically efficient prices subject to the same net revenue constraint with shadow price σ are

$$p_i - C_i' = - \left(\frac{\sigma}{1 + \sigma}\right)\frac{f_i}{f_i'} = - \left(\frac{\sigma}{1 + \sigma}\right)\frac{p_i}{\eta_i} \quad i = 1, 2$$

$$\alpha_3 - C_3' < 0 \tag{8.23}$$

We see from this that for services which are provided the proportionate deviation from marginal cost should be inversely proportional to price elasticity. For instance, if an operating profit has to be raised relative to marginal cost pricing (that is if the profit constraint is binding and $\sigma > 0$) then the margin of fare over marginal cost should be higher in inelastic markets because then least distortion is caused relative to marginal cost pricing. Note that no prices should fall below marginal costs, and that if the profit constraint is not binding (so $\sigma = 0$) then all prices should equal marginal costs. This is in contrast to the passenger miles case where some fares may be above and some below marginal costs. For instance in markets with very high elasticities ($\eta_i \rightarrow - \infty$), (8.20) implies a limiting price *below* marginal cost by an amount $1/\lambda$, whereas (8.23) implies marginal cost pricing. In other words price discrimination and cross-subsidization may be introduced because of a tendency to push the fare on an inelastic service above marginal operating costs, in order to earn surplus revenue which can be used to finance a service which exhibits a relatively high elasticity (and hence easily provides an increase in passenger miles). In fact, a service may be operated for which the *level* of demand (willingness to pay) is never high enough to allow price to cover marginal cost. (From the point of view of the dual, the temptation is to earn extra profit on the inelastic service in order to subsidize the elastic but unprofitable service, so that it will make a good contribution to satisfying the minimum passenger miles constraint.)

We described how the objective of passenger miles maximization could be made operational by instructing decision-makers to compare the marginal costs (savings) of each project, net of the revenue it would generate (lose), with a standard 'pass-mark'. For net social surplus maximization, (8.23) shows that a similar decision rule can be developed. It may be rewritten

$$p_i \left[1 + \left(\frac{\sigma}{1 + \sigma} \right) \frac{1}{\eta_i} \right] - C_i' = 0 \quad i = 1, 2 \qquad (8.24)$$

for a provided service. Implementation requires that the modified marginal revenue be equal to marginal cost, the modification being to increase each elasticity by the constant, $(1 + \sigma)/\sigma$. The constant σ is the extra net social benefit attainable by a £1 increase in subsidy, and it takes the place of the pass-mark. The differences between the approaches are discussed in more detail by Glaister and Collings (1978). That paper also discusses the possibilities of devising systems of weights to be applied to the passenger mileage sold in the different markets so as to make the weighted passenger miles maximization approach equivalent to the economically efficient pricing one.

8.3 The differences implied by differing objectives: an illustration

In this section we illustrate the arguments of earlier sections by presenting the results of numerical calculations. They should be regarded as illustrative only; although the data used are intended to be representative of London Transport's bus and rail services, they are inevitably subject to considerable uncertainty. Throughout this section linear demand relations are used, and in this section time costs are suppressed, and cost is therefore identified with money fare.

Calculations are carried out with two sets of own-price elasticities. In the first, bus elasticity is -0.64 and rail is -0.4, to correspond with the values determined by London Transport (Fairhurst 1975). In the second case bus elasticity is -0.8 and rail is -0.2, to cover the range of $\frac{1}{2}$: 2 quoted by Quarmby (1977, §217).

Marginal costs are assumed constant and equal to 7 and 2 pence per passenger mile for bus and rail respectively. These values are a rough average of most recent results obtained by London Transport (LT) from its bus scheduling model and other sources (see Glaister and Lewis 1978). Demand levels at 1975 fares levels were taken at 27.5×10^6 and 32.5×10^6 passenger miles per five-day week respectively, and shares in total Greater London expenditure were calculated at 0.82% and 0.87% from Family Expenditure Survey and LT data.

Table 8.1 shows the results. For each of a variety of required operating profit levels, Π, it shows the solutions to the first-order conditions for passenger miles maximization (8.22) and the net social surplus maximization (8.24). The value of the pass-mark (i.e. λ) is also given in passenger miles per £, and so is the percentage welfare loss attributable to the difference between the passenger miles maximizing prices and net-social-surplus maximizing prices (the latter prices being the economically efficient solutions). These calculations are repeated for the alternative sets of elasticities. It should be noted that the required 'profits' are what must be provided out of operations as a contribution to cover that part of fixed costs which is not covered by external subsidy.

The following points will be noted: the general properties predicted in previous section are confirmed; passenger miles may give one price above and one below marginal cost, while net consumers' surplus always has both above for positive profits or both below for negative profits; with the second set of elasticities passenger miles maximization gives an interesting 'reversal', $p_1 < p_2$, in spite of the much higher bus marginal cost.

There are numerous large differences between the fares calculated under the two policies, especially with the second, more disparate, pair of elasticities. The extreme reluctance to raise the fare in the more elastic market will be noted in this case. The results are qualitatively similar to those obtained by Nash (1978).

The calculated welfare losses, though variable, are apparently small, except in extreme circumstances. However, this

Table 8.1 Calculations relating to London Transport services

Profit (£m per week)	Profit (£m p.a.)	$\eta_1 = -0.65$ Passenger miles			$\eta_2 = -0.4$ Net social surplus		
		p_1	p_2	Pass-mark*	p_1	p_2	Loss (%)
−1.0	−52.0	3.14	2.57	9	6.48	0.01	0.25
−0.8	−41.6	3.39	2.81	9	6.57	0.35	0.23
−0.6	−31.2	3.65	3.07	10	6.67	0.73	0.21
−0.3	−15.6	4.06	3.48	11	6.82	1.33	0.17
+ 0.2	10.4	4.84	4.27	13	7.13	2.49	0.12
+ 0.3	15.6	5.02	4.45	14	7.19	2.76	0.11
0.4	20.8	5.21	4.63	15	7.26	3.03	0.10
0.6	31.2	5.64	5.04	17	7.42	3.64	0.07
0.8	41.6	6.10	5.52	20	7.61	4.34	0.05
1.0	52.0	6.71	6.14	27	7.83	5.21	0.03
1.15	59.8	7.30	6.72	39	8.08	6.11	0.014
1.25	65.0	8.02	7.44	89	8.34	7.13	0.003

Profit (£m per week)	Profit (£m p.a.)	$\eta_1 = -0.8$ Passenger miles			$\eta_2 = -0.2$ Net social surplus		
		p_1	p_2	Pass-mark*	p_1	p_2	Loss (%)
−1.0	−52.0	0.44	5.45	6.7	6.82	0.01	0.95
−0.8	−41.6	0.63	5.63	6.8	6.85	0.36	0.91
−0.6	−31.2	0.82	5.82	6.9	6.89	0.76	0.86
−0.3	−15.6	1.12	6.12	7.3	6.94	1.37	0.78
+ 0.2	10.4	1.65	6.65	7.8	7.04	2.44	0.66
+ 0.3	15.6	1.76	6.76	8.0	7.06	2.66	0.64
0.4	20.8	1.88	6.88	8.1	7.08	2.89	0.61
0.6	31.2	2.11	7.11	8.5	7.13	3.36	0.57
0.8	41.6	2.35	7.35	8.8	7.16	3.85	0.52
1.0	52.0	2.61	7.61	9.2	7.21	4.36	0.47
1.15	59.8	2.81	7.81	9.6	7.25	4.75	0.44
1.25	65.0	2.94	7.94	9.9	7.27	5.03	0.41

* In passenger miles per £   Source: Glaister and Collings (1978)

conclusion requires caution. In the first place, as argued in chapter 9, the neglect of cross-price elasticities can cause a serious underestimate of true welfare losses — perhaps by a factor of up to five. Secondly, the smallness must be placed in the context of the assumed small proportions of *total* Greater London expenditure represented by bus and tube travel. Thus a loss of say 0.5% of all welfare represents a loss of about $0.005 \div (0.0082 + 0.0087) \times 100 = 29.6\%$ of expenditure on LT public transport. At 1972 prices a 0.5% welfare loss represents about 20p per household per week, or a total of £28.7 million per year. In the case with elasticities in the range $\frac{1}{2}: 2$ mentioned by Quarmby (1977), losses are of this order of magnitude.

8.4 Income redistribution

The discussion so far in this book has subjugated the problem of the effect that pursuing particular objectives might have on the distribution of income, or welfare. As discussed in chapter 4, all that has been required has been the possibility of making a potential *Pareto* improvement. Following some ideas of Feldstein (1972) we now briefly show one way in which considerations of income distribution may be introduced. It is a fundamental prerequisite for this analysis that the weightings to be given to different income groups be chosen. This is, of course, a subjective matter and would normally be considered outside the professional competence of the economist.

Let the average income of individuals using service i be y_i and let $u'(y_i)$ be the social valuation to be attached to the welfare for this group, as a function of y_i. This notation suggests that the weights should be related to the marginal utilities of income of the different groups. However, this only makes sense if utility can be assumed to be a cardinal measure and that the utilities of different individuals can be added, subtracted and compared, as their weights can be. This is a stronger assumption than many economists are prepared to make and it is stronger than the assumption of ordinal utility which characterizes the rest of this book. For the purposes of this section we need only regard $u'(y_i)$ as given, constant weights to be attracted to individuals in group i, with the properties that $u'(y_i) > 0$ and $\Sigma_i u'(y_i) = 1$.

Consider first the problem of maximizing a weighted sum of consumer surpluses subject to a financial constraint:

$$\text{maximize} \quad \sum_i \left(u'(y_i) \int_{p_i}^{\alpha} f_i(z)\, dz + p_i f_i(p_i) \right.$$
$$\left. - C_i(f_i(p_i)) \right) \quad (8.25)$$

$$\text{subject to} \quad \sum_i [p_i f_i(p_i) - C_i(f_i(p_i))] \geqslant \Pi$$

yields

$$p_i - C'_i = - \left(\frac{1 - u'(y_i) + \sigma}{1 + \sigma} \right) \frac{p_i}{\eta_i} \quad (8.26)$$

The problem (8.25) is a straightforward generalization of the one in (5.23) and (5.24). The solution (8.26) is similarly a generalization of (5.29) (reproduced above as (8.23)); indeed it reduces to (5.29) in the special case that $u'(y_i) = 1$. Compared with the 'standard' solution obtained in chapter 5 the price is lowered for those groups which are given a relatively high social valuation. In contrast, if a group is given a zero valuation, $u'(y_i) = 0$, then (8.26) reduces to the condition that profit earned from that group should be maximized.

However, a full analysis of welfare redistribution must take into account the means by which the subsidy Π is to be raised. The following argument illustrates how this might be done; alternative taxation schemes would require different analyses. Following Feldstein (1972) let the number of individuals in group i be n_i and

$$N = \sum_i n_i$$

Suppose that each member of the population must (say through an income independent property tax) pay the same proportion of operating losses:

$$T = \frac{1}{N} \left(\sum_i [C_i(f_i) - p_i f_i(p_i)] + F \right)$$

where F is the system total fixed cost. Net benefit to group i is then

$$\int_{p_i}^{\alpha} f_i(z)\, dz - n_i T$$

and the weighted sum of net benefits can therefore be written

$$\sum_i u'(y_i) \left(\int_{p_i}^{\alpha} f_i(z)\, dz - \frac{n_i}{N} \sum_i [C_i(f_i) - p_i f_i(p_i) + F] \right)$$

where $u'(y_i)$ gives the weight to be attached to group i as before. This is to be maximized without constraint. The first-order conditions are

$$- u'(y_i) f_i(p_i) - \left(\sum_i \frac{n_i u'(y_i)}{N} \right) [(C_i' - p_i) f_i' - f_i] = 0$$

which, with arrangements yields

$$p_i - C_i' = \left(\frac{u'(y_i)}{\sum_i n_i u'(y_i)/N} - 1 \right) \frac{p_i}{\eta_i} \tag{8.27}$$

Note that this simply implies that for groups with a 'social valuation' greater than the average across all individuals, the price will be below marginal cost (since $\eta_i < 0$) and vice versa. If social valuations were independent of income marginal cost pricing would again result, as a special case, because all social valuations would be equal to the average.

The decision rules embodied in (8.27) may alternatively be obtained by maximizing weighted *expenditures* subject to constraint. Consider

$$\text{maximize} \quad \sum_i - W_i p_i f_i(p_i)$$

$$\tag{8.28}$$

$$\text{subject to} \quad \sum_i [p_i f_i(p_i) - C_i(f_i(p_i))] = \Pi$$

The first-order conditions will be

$$p_i - C_i' = - \left(\frac{\omega - (1 + \eta_i) W_i}{\omega} \right) \frac{p_i}{\eta_i} \tag{8.29}$$

where ω is the shadow price on the constraint.

Comparing (8.29) with what is required in (8.27) shows immediately that the weights W_i must be given by

$$W_i = \frac{\omega u'(y_i)}{\Sigma_i n_i u'(y_i)/N} \frac{1}{1 + \eta_i}$$

or

$$W_i = \hat{\omega} \frac{u'(y_i)}{1 + \eta_i} \qquad (8.30)$$

Equation (8.29) can then be written as

$$C_i' - p_i \left(1 + \frac{1}{\eta_i}\right) = -\frac{p_i}{\eta_i} \frac{u'(y_i)}{\Sigma_i n_i u'(y_i)/N} \qquad (8.31)$$

for comparison with distribution-free results.

Equations (8.30) state that the weights on revenues should be proportional both to the inverses of the elasticities increased by unity and to the 'marginal social valuation' of income to the uses of the service, normalized by the weighted average of these valuations. Equation (8.31) says that in projects marginal costs net of marginal revenues should be compared with an 'inverse pass-mark' which is (p_i/η_i) as before, weighted by the normalized distributional weight. Markets which are given a high social valuation relative to the average will have marginal revenues which are small relative to marginal costs.

We have compared and contrasted the implications of a public transport organization operating under a fixed subsidy (or profit) constraint adopting a policy of maximizing the total number of passenger miles that they sell as opposed to the 'classically correct' prescription of some form of marginal cost pricing. We have shown that 'naive' passenger miles maximization will only yield similar results to the socially optimum policy under strong conditions which are known to be violated in many actual transport systems. Illustrative calculations using data representative of London show that the differences between the policies are not trivial, but may lead to significant differences in the net social welfare generated. However, weighting schemes exist to achieve certain objectives in the distribution of welfare. We have attempted to draw attention to weaknesses in the criterion of passenger miles maximization, but we would accept some of the claims that have been made in its favour. As a device for decentralizing decisions it is more easily understood and accepted as a relevant criterion by those who have to operate it. It may well be that the welfare loss caused by the price distortions it introduces in practice are insignificant when set against the waste due to inefficiencies, mismanagement and a failure to relate what is provided to what the public actually wants. If so, its advantages may, in practice, outweigh its drawbacks.

8.5 The choice of service quality

We have concentrated so far on the problem of the choice of fare level at the expense of the problem of the choice of service quality. In fact operators very often have to decide whether to offer a high quality service at a high price or a poorer one at a lower price. In the case of an urban public transport operator there is what has become known as a 'triangular' relationship between price, service level and subsidy level: if any two are determined then the third must follow as a consequence. This is analysed in some detail by Grey (1975). We shall here discuss the problem of the simultaneous fixing of prices and service levels so as to maximize the social benefit objective developed in section 2.9 without the imposition of a constraint on subsidy. The latter constraint could be added straightforwardly by following the technique outlined in section 5.3 for the case when fare alone is to be fixed.

In the case of an operator like the London Transport Executive, fares and service levels have to be fixed for two interdependent markets: buses and railways. As in section 2.9, let p_1 and p_2 be the fares and q_1 and q_2 be the service qualities. Again, for the sake of the argument, we will characterize service quality as time taken per trip. This will principally depend upon service frequency offered in the case of urban services because this directly affects waiting time whilst it is relatively difficult to change speeds.

As in section 2.9 we shall start with a 'base' set of fares and qualities, p_1', p_2', q_1' and q_2', and ask what the optimum p_1'', p_2'', q_1'' and q_2'' should be. Consumer benefits are given by the compensating variation (CV) in (2.51).

A change in fare structures and/or waiting times will normally involve a change in the level of subsidy to the public modes. This in turn must imply a matching change in the income which individuals forego in the form of taxation. The change in subsidy must therefore be subtracted from the CV to obtain the net social benefit:

$$
\begin{aligned}
- CV + [&p_1'' x_1(\mathbf{p}'', \mathbf{q}'', u) + p_2'' x_2(\mathbf{p}'', \mathbf{q}'', u) \\
&- c_1(x_1(\mathbf{p}'', \mathbf{q}'', u), q_1'') - c_2(x_2(\mathbf{p}'', \mathbf{q}'', u), q_2'')] \\
- [&p_1' x_1(\mathbf{p}', \mathbf{q}', u) + p_2' x_2(\mathbf{p}', \mathbf{q}', u) \\
&- c_1(x_1(\mathbf{p}', \mathbf{q}', u), q_1') - c_2(x_2(\mathbf{p}', \mathbf{q}', u), q_2')]
\end{aligned}
$$
$$(8.32)$$

In expression (8.32) CV appears with a negative sign because, in the case of a price rise, the CV will be positive but will represent a disbenefit.

By rearrangement of terms, (8.32) may be interpreted alternatively as the change in consumer surplus plus the change in revenues (the two together being the change in 'willingness to pay') net of the change in resource costs in the public transport sector.

The terms like $c(\mathbf{x}(\mathbf{p}'', \mathbf{q}'', u), \mathbf{q}'')$ represent the assumption that costs on each mode depend both on the number of trips provided and on the quality at which they are provided.

We shall require the following results: equations (2.47) and (2.48) state that

$$
\frac{\partial g}{\partial p_i} = x_i(\mathbf{p}, \mathbf{q}, u) \quad \text{and} \quad \frac{\partial g}{\partial q_i} = \tau x_i(\mathbf{p}, \mathbf{q}, u)
$$

Hence

$$
\frac{\partial x_i}{\partial p_j} = \frac{\partial^2 g}{\partial p_j \partial p_i} = \frac{\partial^2 g}{\partial p_i \partial p_j} = \frac{\partial x_j}{\partial p_i}
$$
$$(8.33)$$

$$
\frac{\partial x_i}{\partial q_j} = \frac{1}{\tau} \frac{\partial^2 g}{\partial q_j \partial q_i} = \frac{1}{\tau} \frac{\partial^2 g}{\partial q_i \partial q_j} = \frac{\partial x_j}{\partial q_i}
$$
$$(8.34)$$

$$\tau \frac{\partial x_i}{\partial p_j} = \frac{\partial^2 g}{\partial p_j \, \partial q_i} = \frac{\partial^2 g}{\partial q_i \, \partial p_j} = \frac{\partial x_j}{\partial q_i} \tag{8.35}$$

Differentiating (8.32) with respect to p_1'' gives the necessary condition

$$-x_1(p_1'', p_2', q_1'', q_2'', u) - \int_{p_2'}^{p_2''} \frac{\partial x_2(p_1'', z, q_1'', q_2'', u)}{\partial p_1} \, dz$$

$$+ x_1(p_1'', p_2'', q_1'', q_2'', u) + p_1'' \frac{\partial x_1}{\partial p_1}$$

$$- \frac{\partial c_1}{\partial x_1} \frac{\partial x_1''}{\partial p_1} - \frac{\partial c_2}{\partial x_2} \frac{\partial c_2''}{\partial p_1} = 0 \tag{8.36}$$

where $x_1'' = x_1(p_1'', p_2'', q_1'', q_2'', u)$, etc. But using (8.33) and evaluating the integral, (8.36) simplifies to

$$p_1'' = \frac{\partial c_1}{\partial x_1} + \frac{\partial c_2}{\partial x_2} \frac{\partial x_2''/\partial p_1}{\partial x_1''/\partial p_1} \tag{8.37}$$

This is simply a restatement that the price of the service should be set equal to the maginal cost of supply, taking into account any transfers to the respective mode from the other mode that may occur as the price is changed. There is a symmetrical expression for p_2''.

Now consider the derivative of the CV in (2.51) with respect to q_1'':

$$\frac{\partial(-CV)}{\partial q_1} = - \int_{p_1'}^{p_2''} \frac{\partial x_1(z, p_1', q_1'', q_2'', u)}{\partial q_1} \, dz$$

$$- \int_{p_2'}^{p_2''} \frac{\partial x_2(p_1'', z, q_1'', q_2'', u)}{\partial q_1} \, dz$$

$$- \tau x_1(p_1', p_2', q_1'', q_2'', u)$$

$$- \int_{q_2'}^{q_2''} \tau \frac{\partial x_2(p_1', p_2', q_1'', z, u)}{\partial q_1} \, dz \tag{8.38}$$

Using the results (8.33), (8.34) and (8.35) and performing the integrations allows (8.38) to be simplified to

$$\frac{\partial(-CV)}{\partial q_1} = -\tau x_1(p_1'', p_2'', q_1'', q_2'', u) \qquad (8.39)$$

Hence the first-order condition obtained setting the derivative of (8.32) with respect to q_1 equal to zero is

$$-\tau x_1(p_1'', p_2'', q_1'', q_2'', u) + \left(p_1'' - \frac{\partial c_1}{\partial x_1}\right)\frac{\partial x_1}{\partial q_1}$$

$$+ (p_2 - c_2)\frac{\partial x_2}{\partial q_1} - \frac{\partial c_1}{\partial q_1} = 0$$

or

$$-\tau x_1'' = \frac{\partial c_1}{\partial q_1} - \left(p - \frac{\partial c_1}{\partial x_1}\right)\frac{\partial x_1}{\partial q_1} - (p_2 - c_2)\frac{\partial x_2}{\partial q_1}$$

$$(8.40)$$

The left-hand side is the marginal benefit of a quality improvement and the right-hand side is the marginal cost. The latter has two components: the direct marginal costs represented by the first term and the indirect costs represented by the other two terms. Note that if there were no cross-price elasticities then (8.37) would imply that these latter two terms would disappear.

In practice one is often not concerned with the problem of finding the full optimum represented by the solution of the rather intractable conditions represented by (8.37) and (8.40). One simply wishes to say whether a proposed package of fares and service changes would be desirable. Then the net benefit expression in (8.32) would provide a basis for a numerical evaluation of such a proposal. Computer programs have been written to do this which include calculations of congestion benefits to other road users. Hence evaluations of fares and service changes can be computed fairly quickly and cheaply, provided the basic information or demand characteristics and costs is available.

8.6 Problems

(1) Suppose a railway faces demands for its passenger and freight services given by

$$q_1 = \alpha_1 p_1^{\beta_1} \quad \text{and} \quad q_2 = \alpha_2 p_2^{\beta_2} \quad \beta_1 < -1, \beta_2 < -1$$

respectively where q_1 is in passenger miles per annum and q_2 is in ton miles per annum. The prices are £p_1 and £p_2 per unit and the constant demand elasticities are β_1 and β_2. Operating costs are given by £$\gamma_1 q_1$ and £$\gamma_2 q_2$ per unit where γ_1 and γ_2 are constants. Central government stipulates a fixed total annual operating profit of £π. Compare and contrast the alternative pricing policies of maximizing: (a) a consumer surplus measure of the 'public interest'; and (b) the total of passenger and ton miles, $q_1 + q_2$. Discuss your solutions, with special reference to the implied cross-subsidies between the services.

(2) The demand for a certain transport service depends both on its price and its quality. The cost of provision depends upon the quantity and the quality. Set up a formal model and use it to indicate how an appropriate authority might determine the frequency and price of a service. Identify the main pieces of information it would need in order to decide and implement its policy.

(3) A certain local authority has identified two distinct and homogeneous groups of users of public transport services in its area, 'the rich' and 'the poor'. The demands for these services per unit time are known to be given by

$$x_1 = f_1(p_1) \quad \text{and} \quad x_2 = f_2(p_2)$$

where p_1 and p_2 are the fares charged to each group. Being concerned both about economic efficiency and the distribution of welfare between the groups it wishes to choose fares so as to maximize

$$W = w_1 s_1 + w_2 s_2 + p_1 f_1(p_1) + p_2 f_2(p_2) - c_1(x_1) - c_2(x_2)$$
$$w_1 + w_2 = 2 \quad w_1 \geqslant 0 \quad w_2 \geqslant 0$$

where w_1 and w_2 are predetermined weights, s_1 and s_2 are consumer surpluses accruing to each group and $c_1(x_1)$ and $c_2(x_2)$ are costs of providing services. This must be done subject to a constraint on the minimum profit (maximum loss) achieved.

Derive the necessary conditions which the optimum fares must satisfy. Analyse and interpret the way in which the optimum fares will vary with the weights chosen and with the fares' elasticities. Briefly discuss the importance of models of this kind in practical decision-making.

9 Intervention: Regulation, Taxation and Subsidy

All industries operate against a background of restrictions of some kind. This concerns such things as health and safety at work, minimum product safety and trades descriptions. In addition many industries are singled out for special treatment with respect to taxation, subsidy and restrictions on the conditions under which they trade. The latter come under the loose head of 'regulation', and the transport industries would seem to be particularly subject to it. We know from chapter 4 that if markets were perfectly competitive and if there were no 'market failure' then there would be no reason to intervene in their operation on the grounds of improving economic efficiency. Further, any unsatisfactory aspects of the distribution of welfare could, in principle, be rectified by an appropriate system of lump sum taxes and subsidies. Our main interest in this chapter is in those types of regulation which are either supposed to compensate for the various sources of market failure or to prevent 'unfairness'. No new analysis is introduced; the intention is to draw together and apply the principles that have been developed earlier. We begin by listing the arguments commonly mentioned in favour of the main forms of regulation to be found in the transport industries together with examples. We end by mentioning some of the arguments against and some of the alternatives.

The subject is a large one with a rapidly developing literature. This chapter can only claim to be the briefest of summaries of some of the main arguments used. More complete statements will be found, for instance, in Foldes (1961),

Posner (1974), Phillips (1975) in Crew and Kleindorfer (1979) and in the references given therein. Current research is reported in many of the journals, with the *Bell Journal of Economics* specializing in this field.

9.1 Tendency to monopoly

We have shown in chapter 3 that if an industry comprises one profit maximizing supplier, or a few suppliers who find it in their interests to collude and behave as if they were a single supplier, the output will be restricted and price will be raised above marginal cost. This is simply economically inefficient and a *Pareto* improvement could be brought about by forcing output to expand, prices to fall whilst compensating the owners of the monopoly rights. This is one of the simplest and commonest justifications for intervention. Legislation may be enacted to enforce minimum service levels (for example minimum service frequencies) or maximum fares although this may be very difficult to enforce, especially in the case of international movements such as shipping and air travel.

As an alternative to price and quality controls (in some cases in addition to them) attempts have sometimes been made to limit the rate of return on capital employed. This is analysed in detail by Crew and Kleindorfer (1979) who show how this may lead to what has become known as the Averch and Johnson effect whereby capital in overutilized and labour underutilized relative to any cost minimizing solution. Rees (1976) discusses the conflicts that can arise when simultaneous attempts are made to regulate pricing, output, investment criteria and profitability targets, as recent UK Nationalized Industries White Papers would seem to require.

We have seen that one feature of monopoly behaviour is the tendency to price discriminate, i.e. to charge different prices to different groups of users for essentially the same service. Besides being inefficient this has attracted the attention of regulators on the grounds that it is unfair. Unfortunately the extension of this idea of equity has on many occasions led to the imposition of charges which fail to reflect genuine variations of marginal costs of carrying the traffic. Thus regulated railway freight rate fixing has tradi-

tionally adhered to a principle of relating charges to the value
of the goods involved which is very often inversely related to
the costs of carriage. Similarly it was only relatively recently
that the British railway system felt able to charge passengers
different rates per mile for different types of trip; and even
now the variations employed have more to do with competing carriers and price discrimination than cost variation.
There is, for instance, considerable opposition to the idea of
charging peak suburban travellers their true marginal costs
on the grounds that it would be unfair to 'penalize' them.
The Traffic Commissioners, who in the UK administer the
licensing of all public road vehicle services, have similarly
seen fit to enforce more or less uniform pricing on stage
carriage bus services although this was never an explicit
requirement of the terms of the 1930 and subsequent Acts
under which they operate.

Monopolies or cartels may exist for a variety of reasons.
An important one is increasing returns to scale. This will lead
to average costs falling with output so that one large organization will make a larger profit than the joint profit of two
small ones; this is the case of the 'natural monopoly'. In
debates about the desirability of relaxing regulation which
has grown up over the years it is important to attempt to
establish whether increasing returns exist, because if they do
there will be a tendency to natural monopoly. Public intervention may then be thought necessary so as to curb monopolistic pricing behaviour, but not necessarily to break the
monopoly into multiple enterprises.

As we argued in chapter 3, if returns to scale are increasing
up to and beyond the extent of market demand then
marginal costs will be below average costs. Then the efficient
solution can only be achieved by some form of intervention
which involves the payment of subsidy together with the
specification of pricing rules. Typically this is done under
some form of public ownership; the most commonly quoted
example here is the railways although they ran successfully
as private oligopolies subject to price controls for most of
their lives, and there is some dispute about how fixed a large
proportion of their costs really are so that long run marginal
costs might in fact be close to average costs. Another classic

example is the bridge or road whose short run marginal costs are zero and which are therefore provided without charge and financed from general taxation. Again, however, it is often forgotten that in the very long run – in particular in the provision of new facilities – there is often considerable flexibility in the scale of provision. That implies positive long run marginal costs and provides a case for charging a toll (see section 5.2). In any case there may be the elementary case of section 5.1 for charging tolls for the use of congested facilities.

In the absence of increasing returns to scale the long term existence of monopoly or a cartel must rely on some form of barrier to entry of newcomers. Examples are the rights held by the owners of patents on new inventions and the existence of a stock of 'goodwill' amongst the public for established operators together with the expense faced by a newcomer in making his services known. More aggressive tactics are available to such cartels as the shipping liner conferences, e.g. loyalty discounts to customers and the use of financial reserves to run 'fighting ships' for periods at a rate low enough to undercut the incipient newcomer and put him out of business (see Bennathan and Walters 1969). It appears that there may have been some unsuccessful attempts to try this sort of tactic during the recent weakening of the cartel arrangements on the North Atlantic air routes.

Paradoxically, one of the most common sources of monopoly is provided by regulations themselves. For instance the Post Office is protected by law from competition from other mail or telecommunications carriers. Taxi cab law grants the exclusive right to holders of licences to ply for hire in the street. To obtain a licence a driver will have to meet requirements which are often stringent and he may have to pay a very substantial premium for one if, as in most places except London, the numbers issued are limited. Under the provision of the 1930 Road Traffic Act the UK Traffic Commissioners, in deciding whether or not to grant licences for bus services, were to take into account (amongst other things) 'the extent, if any, to which the needs of the proposed routes or any of them are already adequately served ... The co-ordination of all forms of passenger transport including by rail ...'. They were also to have regard that 'fares shall be so fixed as to prevent wasteful competition with alternative forms of transport...'. It is not surprising that these terms of reference have led to the maintenance of monopoly or near monopoly of provision by the railways or by established road operators, both of whom have been keen objectors to proposed new services. This in spite of the fact that it is difficult in the absence of increasing returns to scale to given an objective meaning to a phrase like 'wasteful competition' within the welfare economics framework presented in chapter 4. It is also difficult to assess 'need' other than by the test of whether a service can be sustained by the demand that is forthcoming under competitive conditions.

9.2 Safety

One reason sometimes given for explicitly awarding the benefits of protected monopoly is as a compensation for the additional costs which operators are forced to bear because of other aspects of regulation, such as safety requirements. This is an historically very important reason for the existence of regulation. In fact a large proportion of the current regulation of railway, road and air public service vehicles can be traced to periods when these modes experienced high accident rates during their early years of operation. The market failure that is postulated here is essentially one of failure of perfect information. The user, it is argued, is incapable of correctly perceiving the risks involved and is therefore incapable of signalling his willingness to pay more for the operator who adopts safer equipment or working methods. Nor are the law of compensation or compulsory insurance schemes thought adequate to ensure that the operator will, on his own initiative, choose the appropriate degree of safety so as to balance the risk of compensation claims or the cost of insurance premiums 'correctly' against the considerable extra financial cost which safety measures can involve. In practice it is unusual to find those who administer safety regulations thinking in terms of the trade-off between the public benefits of greater safety and the higher prices they or the taxpayer have to pay in order to secure it. There is typically an overriding concern to achieve absolute safety irrespective of the feasibility or cost of doing so. For instance, there is a long list of safety and manoeuvrability requirements which a vehicle must satisfy before it can be used as a London taxi cab which in effect mean that a specialist vehicle must be used. In addition it must be maintained to an extremely high standard to pass annual and random inspections. At the same time most authorities in other cities find that normal production vehicles are adequate with various degree of inspection and supervision. Little work seems to have been done on the impact of these regulations on safety records or on the economic costs and benefits of them.

9.3 Imperfect information, risk and uncertainty

Failures of perfect information are said to justify other kinds of intervention. Monitoring of service quality may be necessary because, in the short run at least, individuals may be unable to detect changes in such things as reliability, rather as they need to be protected by weights and measures legislation from producers who might surreptitiously reduce the quantities in their packaging. The prepublication and display of fare scales and even the installation of taxi meters and the central fixing of fare levels are all held to be necessary to protect the innocent or ignorant customer from 'exploitation' due to the temporary 'monopoly power' held by the driver of the vehicle he has boarded. At the same time one notes that in most places a completely unregulated 'minicab' trade apparently operates without difficulty whilst arranging all its fares by private treaty. Licensing authorities often require the publication of timetables on the grounds that this enables users to save waiting time by better organizing their activities. They require them to be adhered to because of the detriment suffered by users if their legitimate expectations are not fulfilled. One would have expected, however, that given the freedom to fix prices the operators would find it in their interest to do these things spontaneously because they would be able to extract their value through the fare they receive.

In some cases regulatory bodies feel that as long experienced and chosen professionals in their field they have greater managerial and entrepeneurial skills than the operators themselves, particularly if the trade is composed of a great number of small operators. For instance, it may be thought that they have better access to forecasts about an uncertain future and have specialist skills in producing and interpreting such forecasts. They may then issue directives concerning investment and scrapping, perhaps by imposing rules about the allowable vintages of the vehicles used.

The presence of risk and uncertainty poses a whole series of problems which are outside the simple framework of chapter 4; it is a subject on its own. We will give it no further attention here beyond saying that the authorities have an interest in intervention because of imperfections in capital and insurance markets, because of the tendency for the individual or the small company to exhibit an aversion towards taking risks, and because of the reductions in the costs associated with risk bearing that can be achieved through the pooling of many risks or the sharing of one risk amongst many individuals. The development of a large new aircraft type is an example where the risks are sometimes thought too great for private enterprise to bear. Rees (1976), Heggie (1972), Dorfman (1962), Arrow and Lind (1970) and Crew and Kleindorfer (1979), all have useful discussion of the problems posed for decision-taking by risk and uncertainty.

9.4 Coordination and unfair competition

Regulators such as the Traffic Commisssioners see it as a part of their duties to secure the coordination of operators' services for the public benefit. This typically involves the interlinking of timetables and the imposition of common fare scales on common parts of routes — or indeed the prohibition of the picking up and putting down of passengers by one operator on a part of a route which is served by another. It is sometimes dificult to see why such intervention is necessary since, if something is in the interest of the public, it will also be in the interests of the operator seeking to maximize his patronage. It may certainly be the case that there is a need for an agency to point out possibilities for rationalization and to act as a general 'clearing house' for information. There may also be a need for an 'arbitration and conciliation' service to provide a forum at which difficult and acrimonious disputes can be settled, especially as they may involve complicated multilateral negotiations. But this is something less than a quasi-judicial traffic court where independent commissioners impose a decision made according to criteria to which no party to the dispute would necessarily subscribe.

There is one difficulty which has been observed to occur concerning timetables which regulation can successfully overcome. On an infrequently served route a perceptive operator will realize advantages to his passengers and to his own trade of publishing a timetable. But it is then open to a 'pirate' operator to run just ahead of the timetable and 'steal' many of his passengers. The result may be a reluctance to publish a timetable with the attendant lost benefit to the public. Forcing all operators to work to a declared published timetable solves this problem.

We have already mentioned the view that the notion of 'wasteful competition' is a difficult one to formulate in the absence of increasing returns to scale of some sort. There are undoubtedly cases where things like indivisibilities and network effects do mean that one operator can provide a given level of service more cheaply than two, and one would expect such a situation to develop into a natural monopoly in the absence of regulation. But there is sometimes a tendency to regard any situation where a service is duplicated as wasteful whilst neglecting the virtues of the competitive process.

This appears sometimes to be because of a tendency to see things from the point of view of an established operator who has something to lose from a new competitor to the neglect of the user who might have been offered a better quality service at a lower cost – or at least one more suited to his own particular preferences – as a result of having a variety of competing services.

The notion of 'unfair competition' is similarly rather a vague one. Often the phrase is used to refer to situations where one operator is claimed to be having to meet costs that a competitor escapes. Thus railways have long complained that they have to meet all their own infrastructure costs whilst competing coach services are provided with free road space by the state. Whilst this argument has carried some weight over the years one objection to it from the point of view of the principles of efficiency that we have outlined in chapter 4 is that a service should be provided at its long run *marginal* cost and the track costs of both modes are typically rather independent of marginal services. If coach users are willing to pay sufficient to cover the marginal costs of their trip then they should be allowed to do so and the two modes will be competing 'fairly' by the criterion of the efficient allocation of resources.

The notion of fairness is also sometimes employed when there is a desire to protect an operator for some special reason, such as a nascent domestic airline. Any subsidy given by foreign governments to their own operators — say in connection with the carriage of the mails — then attracts a charge of unfair competition.

9.5 Cross-subsidy

It is an explicit requirement that some regulatory agencies should act in such a way as to force operators to provide services which are unremunerative but which are thought to be in the public interest. This is achieved by making the grant of licences to operate the remunerative services conditional on the consent of the operator to provide the others. The fare fixed for the profitable service may contain a mark-up to provide sufficient extra revenue to cover the losses incurred elsewhere. This must necessarily involve a departure from marginal cost pricing principles in the unremunerative market and may mean the same in profit making ones if there is otherwise insufficient 'excess' profit available. There will inevitably be welfare losses relative to the economically efficient policy. We have illustrated in section 8.2, in the context of the cross-subsidies which may be induced by passenger miles maximization, how these might be estimated and that in principle they may be large. The failure to enforce peak price premiums will also cause (largely unconscious) cross-subsidy within a route between users at different times of day.

In circumstances such as this the licensing system is often explicitly used to provide a monopoly to the operator on the more lucrative parts of his system in compensation for forcing him to provide the non-lucrative services. The activity of those who would seek to compete for the attractive trade is sometimes called 'cream-skimming' and any attempt at it stimulates the most bitter complaints from the established operator. Note however that the concept of cream-skimming only has any meaning in the context of a system of fare fixing and licensing which causes cross-subsidy to occur. Otherwise, in terms of our idealized model of chapter 4, competition would cause each market or sub-market to be treated on its merits, fares being driven to long run marginal costs. Regulation very often leads to the anomalous situation where the most jealously guarded rights are those to serve the peak although these are in fact the most expensive to serve.

The cross-subsidy system can cause particular difficulties to the industry involved if, because of a declining overall demand for the service to which the regulatory process is slow to react, the system as a whole becomes unprofitable. It is arguable for instance that in the UK the system worked quite well for stage carriage bus services between its inception in 1930 and the mid-1950s when demand was generally buoyant. Since then however there has been a steady decline in demand. It is likely that the industry has had to contract more quickly and bigger subsidies from central funds have been necessary than would have been the case in the absence of cross-subsidy.

An argument in favour of the system is that it provides an administratively cheap and simple way of securing non-commercial services because one is effectively persuading the operator himself to act as a collector of the taxes which are required to provide the necessary subsidy.

9.6 Externalities

We have argued at length that externalities such as congestion and noise will cause economic inefficiency unless they are internalized by means of a tax or subsidy. Typically such fiscal measures are not used and regulations are imposed as a partial substitute. Thus aircraft have to observe noise reduction procedures and are limited in the times of day that they can operate. Similarly congestion reduction has been advanced as a justification for limiting the numbers of licences issued to taxis in many cities. 'Second best' arguments may also be involved.

9.7 Dynamic instabilities

It is argued that stability is of itself desirable and that the price mechanism will fail to yield it. The arguments here are many and complex; Foldes (1961) gives a summary and evaluation of them.

9.8 National considerations

Many forms of intervention originate in national policy. For instance price controls may be introduced as part of counter-inflation policy. There may be a desire to protect employment so the use of domestically produced equipment may be specified or competition against particularly large nationalized employers may be discouraged. There may be a desire to redistribute welfare; by enforcing concessions to the disabled and elderly for instance. (Rees 1976 has a good discussion of these considerations in the context of the UK public enterprises). There may be matters of national prestige which dictate that certain equipment be produced and used; the supersonic airliner is perhaps an example of this.

9.9 Theories of regulation

We have now listed many of the ostensible reasons for regulation in terms of the various 'corrections' that may be necessary to the competitive process. We now very briefly mention some of the more general ideas that have been put forward as to the real functions that regulation serves.

In the context of domestic air transport policy Foldes (1961) advances the hypotheses that controls are 'designed to enable the government to secure at the least possible cost to public funds, certain facilities and services required in connection with its policies' (p. 156). He has in mind 'Needs of military and other departments of government, social services, control of congestion of airspace and airports and resource allocation'. He goes on to argue that most of the relevant regulations could be explained by this hypothesis.

In a very useful critique R. A. Posner (1974) lists three theories. The first broadly following from the arguments we have already listed is 'the public interest theory'. In its original form 'one assumption was that economic markets are extremely fragile and apt to operate very inefficiently (or inequitably) if left alone; the other was that government regulation is virtually costless'. A reformulation in the face of evidence – especially evidence against the costlessness assumption – holds that 'regulatory agencies are created for *bona fide* public purposes, but then are mismanaged, with the result that those purposes are not always achieved'. Against this he argues that the evidence is consistent with a rival view that 'the typical regulatory agency operates with reasonable efficiency to attain deliberately inefficient or inequitable goals set by the legislature that created it'.

Posner calls the second theory the 'capture theory'. One version is that 'regulation is not about the public interest at all, but is a process by which interest groups seek to promote their (private) interests'. Another version derives from political science and emphasizes the importance of interest groups in the formation of public policy, suggesting that 'over time regulatory agencies come to be dominated by the industries regulated' (p. 341).

The third theory is the 'economic theory' proposed by George Stigler. 'It discards the unexplained, and frequently untrue, assumption of pristine legislative purpose; it admits the possibility of "capture" by interest groups other than the regulated firms; and it replaces the "capture" metaphor ... by the more neutral terminology of supply and demand. But it insists with the political scientists that economic regulation

serves the private interests of politically effective groups.'
'The theory is based on two simple but important insights.
The first is that since the coercive power of the government
can be used to give valuable benefits to particular individuals
or groups, economic regulation — the expression of that
power in the economic sphere — can be viewed as product
whose allocation is governed by laws of supply and demand.'
This 'directs attention to factors bearing on the value of regulation to particular groups of individuals or groups, since,
other things being equal, we can expect a product to be
supplied to those who value it most' ... 'The second insight
is that the theory of cartels may help us to locate the demand
and supply curves'.

The 'analysis suggests that while the characteristics that
predispose an industry to successful cartelisation may also
help it to obtain favourable government regulation, one
characteristic that discourages cartelisation — a large number
of parties whose cooperation is necessary to create and maintain the cartel — encourages regulation. Large numbers have
voting (and potentially, coercive) power and also increase the
likelihood of an asymmetry of interests that will encourage
broad participation in the coalition seeking regulation. In
addition, large numbers, and other factors that discourage
private cartelisation, increase the demand for protective
legislation. The economic theory can thus be used to explain
why we so often observe protective legislation in areas like
agriculture, labour, and the professions, where private cartelisation would hardly be feasible.'

After reviewing the available evidence Posner concludes
that of the public interest and economic theories neither 'can
be said to have, as yet, substantial empirical support. Indeed,
neither theory has been refined to the point where it can
generate hypotheses sufficiently precise to be verified
empirically. However, the success of the economic theory
in illuminating other areas of non-market behaviour leads one
to be somewhat optimistic that the economic theory will jell:
the general assumption of economics that human behaviour
can best be understood as the response of rational self-
interested beings to their environment must have extensive
application to the political process'.

9.10 The costs of regulation

Having identified some of the supposed benefits of and reasons for regulation we now mention some of the disadvantages. The costs may be divided into two main groups. On the one hand there are the direct costs of staffing the regulatory agencies and courts and the direct costs to the operators of higher vehicle and maintenance standards, litigation and so on. In principle these costs ought to be relatively easy to estimate although one must not forget to include a certain amount (and possibly a great deal) of unseen 'out of court' activity in the calculation. In fact rather few such calculations seem to have been carried out.

The second group of costs may be generally termed misallocation costs caused when, far from correcting market failures and distortions regulation actually causes them. Leibenstein (1966), Harberger (1954) and others argued that the actual welfare losses that are likely to occur because of price distortions are very small, and insignificant when compared to the losses caused by waste and mismanagement: so called X-efficiency. It has been argued more recently that their calculations involved unrealistic assumptions concerning the magnitudes of the elasticities involved, the degree of substitutability or complementarity between goods and other matters. Bergson (1973) showed by numerical example how the calculations could be in error. I attempted to generalize Bergson's results (Glaister 1979) and showed that if the approximate welfare loss L, expressed as a proportion of total consumer expenditure, is defined by

$$L = \frac{\mathbf{p}^* \mathbf{x}(\mathbf{p}, u) - g(\mathbf{p}^*, u)}{g(\mathbf{p}^*, u)} \qquad (9.1)$$

where $\mathbf{p}^*$ is the vector of efficient prices and $g(\mathbf{p}, u)$ is the expenditure function defined in (2.30) and aggregated over all individuals, then

$$L \simeq -\tfrac{1}{2} \sum_i \sum_j \gamma_i \eta_{ij} \rho_i \rho_j \qquad (9.2)$$

where γ_i is the fraction of income spent on the ith good, η_{ij} is the elasticity of demand for good i with respect to the price of good j, and ρ_i is the proportionate deviation of the actual regulated price from the economically efficient one. The approximation in (9.2) shows that the welfare losses will depend in a quite general fashion on the precise way in which the own-price elasticities, price distortions, and expenditure shares interact – as Bergson also demonstrated. They show that the loss equally involves the corresponding cross-price elasticities between goods.

London underground fares were increased in the thirty-seventh week of 1972 and then both bus and underground fares remained unchanged until the twelfth week of 1975. During this time the retail price index rose from 100.00 to 144.1 and an index of earnings rose somewhat more than this. Therefore real fares fell substantially during a period when, other things being equal, they should have been increased slightly. On the assumption that the fares were at their optimum levels at the beginning of this period we now use the above equation together with some illustrative data gathered by Lewis and myself (Glaister and Lewis 1978) to estimate the rate of welfare loss associated with this period of price restraint.

The *Family Expenditure Survey* shows that in 1972 total expenditure in Greater London at current prices was £105 million per week, of which about 1.12% was spent on bus services and 1.11% on London Transport rail. Table 9.1 shows a set of own- and cross-fare compensated elasticities derived by aggregation from table 9.2 which is explained later. Substituting these values in the approximation with $\rho_1 = \rho_2 = -0.306$ gives a welfare loss of 0.02%. At 1972 prices this represents about 0.7p per household per week, or a total of £1.1 million per year for the whole Greater London area. This is about 0.9% of total revenue from the two

Table 9.1

	Demand for	
	Bus	Rail
Bus fare	−0.43	0.15
Rail fare	0.16	−0.34

modes. Although this is a small quantity it comes from distortions in the prices of commodities which form a very small proportion of total expenditure. This is because London Transport's services form a small proportion of total transport expenditure in the area, which is about 13% of all expenditure on average. If this exercise were to be repeated for the whole of the transport sector – or indeed for all components of expenditure – then the welfare losses might be substantial. However, one cannot escape the conclusion that the losses caused by price 'distortion' (as measured here) in London Transport's fares due to price restraint over this period were not large. In fact failure to maintain real wages contributed to a staff shortage which caused a serious deterioration in service quality. This may well have caused a much more significant welfare loss. Traffic congestion externalities are ignored in this calculation and they too may be significant.

During 1975 there were two fares increases which succeeded in restoring real bus fares to roughly what they had been at the beginning of 1970 and increasing real underground fares somewhat above previous levels. In 1976 both fares were about 4.3p per passenger mile on average. On the other hand, as described in section 5.5, Lewis and I calculated an 'optimum' set of peak and off-peak bus and rail fares when marginal social costs and cross-price elasticities between private and public transport are taken into account. The set of compensated elasticities, derived from various sources, is shown in table 9.2. The table also shows the 'optimum' fares (from table 5.4), the proportionate distortions of actual 1976 fares from these optima ρ, and the predicted shares of expenditure at the optimum γ.

With these parameter values the formula gives an estimated welfare loss of 2.99%. If, however, peak and off-peak data are aggregated to give just two services, bus and rail, then we obtain proportionate price distortions of -0.27 and 0.36 respectively, expenditure shares 0.0086 and 0.019 and the set of elasticities shown in table 9.1. The equation then estimates the welfare loss at 0.0765%.

Aggregating further to give just one aggregate public transport service gives a price distortion of 0.16, an expenditure

Table 9.2

Elasticities with respect to:	Bus		Rail	
	Peak	Off-peak	Peak	Off-peak
Bus fare				
Peak	−0.35	0.04	0.14	0.01
Off-peak	0.029	−0.87	0.009	0.28
Rail fare				
Peak	0.143	0.013	−0.30	0.05
Off-peak	0.008	0.28	0.018	−0.75
Optimum fares (pence)	7.02	3.12	6.11	0.54
ρ	−0.40	0.35	−0.31	6.67
γ	0.0072	0.0015	0.017	0.0018

share of 0.027 and an elasticity of − 0.22. The equation then estimates the welfare loss at 0.00796%.

The purpose of this exercise is simply to illustrate how aggregation of commodities which should truly be regarded as separate can lead to underestimation of welfare losses, and therefore to suggest that those who have dismissed the importance of allocative efficiency in favour of the X-inefficiency argument may have done so too readily. However, one caveat should be entered. The expression given in (9.2) is an approximation to the 'true' loss. In the fully disaggregate case some of the price distortions are sufficiently large to cast doubt on the accuracy of this approximation. The averaging procedure implicit in the aggregation makes this less of a problem for the more aggregate cases.

The numerical calculations presented here are really only intended as illustrations. As propositions about London Transport's pricing policy they must be treated with reserve. There are many difficulties but I mention two. First, the assumption that the 'base' prices are indeed the optimum prices is debatable, especially in the case of the price restraint argument. Second, the approximations involved may not be valid and to be exact one would need to know the forms of the demand functions, as Bergson did by assumption, and to work out explicit forms for the welfare losses. Other calculations yield similar results.

Chapter 5 illustrates how failure to adopt peak pricing in one example — and thereby to use the off-peak traffic to cross-subsidize the peak — would have led to the overall rate of operating profit being reduced to between three-quarters and one-half what it otherwise would have been (although one cannot directly relate this to an actual economic welfare loss of course). Chapter 8 illustrates the kind of losses that cross-subsidy induced by the objective of passenger miles maximization might cause.

Beesley (1973b, 1979) has discussed regulation as it affects the suppliers of taxi cab services and Beesley and Glaister (1981) have discussed the problems faced by regulators of taxi cab trades when the interests of the consumer are taken into account. To mention some other case studies, Eads (1975) considers the hypothesis that any competition amongst airlines on a given route is wasteful, if fares are fixed by a regulating authority. He discusses an interesting but simplistic model of non-price competition, illustrating the pressures which lead to an overprovision of capacity and a service quality which is higher than the 'optimum' from the consumer point of view. He shows that with random passenger arrivals the optimum in terms of balancing the costs of average passenger waiting plus travel times against increasing costs of higher service frequencies would dictate moderately high load factors which should increase with route length. In fact some rather sketchy data show that in the regulated US domestic market load factors typically declined with distance for longer distances and that routes with several carriers achieved much poorer load factors than monopoly markets over all distances. European carriers are criticized for squandering the potential benefits of pooling arrangements through technical and managerial inefficiency. He concludes that regulated fares require strict regulation of services offered by carriers. But his preferred solution would be to deregulate completely and allow competitive forces to determine fares and service qualities (but not safety standards). Successful experience of this kind of operation in Californian intrastate markets is cited, and it will be interesting to assess the national experience after the large measure of deregulation that has occurred more recently.

Moore (1975) gives an estimate of the allocative inefficiency caused by the chaotic state of American regulation in surface freight transportation. These have had to be rough calculations, but they indicated that possibly one-third of all income generated in this industry is wasted. It may be added that there are reasons for suspecting that his estimate of the consumer surplus losses may be much too low because of the significant cross-price elasticities between modes which may indicate aggregation errors for the kind of reason that has already been given.

Further arguments against regulation are as follows. The administrative process, which often involves the paraphernalia of courts and litigation can be very cumbersome and slow and so impede the innovation of new services. Further, regulations and their agencies tend to outlive their usefulness and remain to impede progress as the technology and the conditions of demand develop. We have already noted in section 9.5 how the enforcement of cross-subsidy in the stage carriage bus service in the UK by the Traffic Commissioners may have worked well enough in the earlier years but have been causing increasing and possibly unnecessary contraction of services recently as the demand has declined and the remunerative services have been less able to support the others. Similarly recent high rates of inflation have caused particular difficulties because of the unwillingness of price regulators to respond sufficiently quickly so that fares fall substantially in real terms quite unintentionally. London came to require a specialized vehicle as a taxi cab because the vehicle specifications, which had been drawn up in the very early days of the motor vehicle before the First War to exclude certain unsuitable domestic models, remained in force long after the War. But technology had changed rapidly by then and none of the much improved production vehicles could meet certain of the old specifications (see Georgano 1972). The Public Carriage Office of the Metropolitan Police was, until 1933, responsible for certification of London bus as well as taxi design. There was a period of several years before 1926 when they refused to allow either kind of vehicle to use four wheel braking systems on the grounds that it might make them pull up too sharply. Barker and Robbins (1974) relate many similar examples.

It is sometimes argued that the tasks that regulators are given are very often either very vaguely defined or impossible to achieve and that the typical response to failure is to expand and compound the regulations. Put into the position of the 'expert' with both the power and the responsibility to take decisions according to ill-defined criteria of public interest and fairness, there is an inevitable tendency over a period to develop views and establish a body of 'case law' which may be quite different from what the original legislation intended. Reading the reports of the Traffic Commissioners over the period 1930 to 1939 gives a very strong impression of this phenomenon (Mulley 1981).

Further complications arise because of the common procedure of requiring those who propose new services to 'prove' need in the face of objections from established operators. This inevitably favours the latter especially if they are large, well organized, employ specialist advocates and if their cooperation is necessary for controls to work smoothly.

Finally, even without these objections there are often very severe theoretical difficulties of prediction and evaluation of the impacts of regulations especially where service quality is involved. If the theoretical problems can be satisfactorily resolved there remains the very severe problem that there are rarely enough data available to allow the estimation of the required quantities, such as price and service quality elasticities and cost conditions in the industry. Beesley and Glaister (1981) have discussed these problems in the context of the taxi trades.

Bibliography

Abelson, P. W. and Flowerdew, A. D. J. (1972), Roskill's successful recommendation, *J. R. Statist. Soc.*

Advisory Committee on Trunk Road Assessment (1977) (Chairman: Sir George Leitch), *Report,* October (London: HMSO)

Advisory Committee on Trunk Road Assessment (1979a), *Trunk Road Proposals – A Comprehensive Framework for Appraisal,* October (London: HMSO)

Advisory Committee on Trunk Road Assessment (1979b) (Chairman: Sir George Leitch), *Forecasting Traffic on Trunk Roads: A Report on the Regional Highway Traffic Model Project,* December (London: HMSO)

Apostol, T. (1957), *Mathematical Analysis* (Reading, Mass.: Addison Wesley)

Arrow, K. J. and Lind, R. C. (1970), Uncertainty and the evaluation of public investment decisions, *Am. Economic Rev.*

Atkinson, A. B. and Stiglitz, J. E. (1980), *Lectures on Public Economics* (Maidenhead: McGraw-Hill)

Bailey, N. T. J. (1957), *The Mathematical Theory of Epidemics* (London: Griffin)

Bailey, N. T. J. (1964), *The Elements of Stochastic Processes* (New York: Wiley)

Barker, T. C. and Robbins, M. (1974), *A History of London Transport,* Vol. II (London: George Allen and Unwin)

Bates, J., Gunn, H. and Roberts, M. (1978), *A Disaggregate Model of Household Car Ownership* (London: Department of Transport)

Baumol, W. J. and Bradford, P. F. (1970), Optimal departures from marginal cost pricing, *Am. Economic Rev.*

Beesley, M. E. (1965), The value of time spent in travelling: some new evidence, *Economica*

Beesley, M. E. (1973a), *Urban Transport: Studies in Economic Policy* (London: Butterworths)

Beesley, M. E. (1973b), Regulation of taxis, *Economic J.*, March

Beesley, M. E. (1979), Competition and supply in London taxis, *J. Transport Economics and Policy*, January

Beesley, M. E. and Glaister, S. (1981), Criteria for the regulation of taxis. Mimeograph

Bennathan, E. and Walters, A. A. (1969), *The Economics of Ocean Freight Rates* (New York: Praeger)

Bergson, A. (1973), On monopoly welfare losses, *Am. Economic Rev.*, December

Bly, P. H. (1976), The effect of fares on bus patronage, *Crowthorne, Transport and Road Research Laboratory Report* LR733

Borins, S. F. (1978), Pricing and investment in a transportation network: the case of Toronto airport, *Can. J. Economics*, November

British Road Federation (1979), *Basic Road Statistics 1979* (London: British Road Federation)

Bruzelius, N. (1979), *The Value of Travel Time* (London: Croom Helm)

Chisholm, M. and O'Sullivan, P. (1973), *Freight Flows and Spatial Aspects of the British Economy* (Cambridge: Cambridge University Press)

Committee of Inquiry into Operator's Licensing (1979) (Chairman, C. D. Foster) (London: HMSO)

Cox, D. R. and Smith, W. L. (1961), *Queues* (London: Chapman and Hall)

Crew, M. A. and Kleindorfer, P. R. (1979), *Public Utility Economics* (London: Macmillan)

Currie, J. M., Murphy, J. A. and Schmitz, A. (1971), The concept of economic surplus and its use in economic analysis, *Economic J.*

Deaton, A. and Muellbauer, J. (1980), *Economics and Consumer Behaviour* (Cambridge: Cambridge University Press)

Debreu, G. (1959), *Theory of Value* (Yale: Cowles Foundation)

Department of Transport (1980a), COBA, version 8 (London: Department of Transport)

Department of Transport (1980b), *National Road Traffic Forecasts*, July

Domencich, T. A. and McFadden, D. (1975), *Urban Travel Demand* (Amsterdam: North Holland)

Dorfman, R. (1962), Basic economic and technologic concepts, in *Design of Water Resource Systems*, A. Maass *et al.* (Eds) (Harvard: Harvard University Press)

Dorfman, R., Samuelson, P. and Solow, R. (1958), *Linear Programming and Economic Analysis* (New York: McGraw-Hill)

Dupuit, J. (1844), Public works and the consumer, reprinted in *Transport*, D. Munby (Ed.) (Harmondsworth: Penguin)

Eades, G. C. (1975), Competition in the domestic trunk airline industry: too much or too little?, in *Promoting Competition in Regulated Markets*, A. Phillips (Ed.) (Washington: Brookings Institution)

Fairhurst, M. H. (1975), Variations in the demand for bus and rail travel in London up to 1974, *Economic Research Report* R210, *London Transport*

Feldstein, M. S. (1972), Equity and efficiency in public pricing, *Q. J. Economics*, May

Fitzgerald, E. V. K. and Aneuryn-Evans, G. B. (1973), The economics of airport development and control, *J. Transport Economics and Policy*, September

Foldes, L. P. (1961), Domestic air transport policy, *Economica*, May, August

Foster, C. D. (1963), *The Transport Problem* (London: Blackie)

Foster, C. D. (1971), *Politics, Finance and the Role of Economics* (London: George Allen and Unwin)

Friedman, M. (1949), The Marshallian demand curve, *J. Political Economy*, December

Gale, D. (1960), *The Theory of Linear Economic Models* (New York: McGraw-Hill)

Georgano, G. N. (1972), *A History of the London Taxicab* (Newton Abbott: David and Charles)

Giles, G. E. and Worsley, T. E. (1979), Development of methods for forecasting car ownership and use, *Economic Trends*, August

Glaister, S. (1974), Consumer surplus and public transport pricing, *Economic J.*, December

Glaister, S. (1976), Peak load pricing and the channel tunnel, *J. Transport Economics and Policy*, May

Glaister, S. (1978), *Mathematical Methods for Economists*, 2nd edn (Oxford: Basil Blackwell)

Glaister, S. (1979), On the estimation of disaggregate welfare losses with an application to price distortions in urban transport, *Am. Economic Rev.*, September

Glaister, S. and Collings, J. J. (1978), Passenger-miles maximization in theory and practice, *J. Transport Economics and Policy*, September

Glaister, S. and Lewis, D. L. (1978), An integrated fares policy for transport in Greater London, *J. Public Economics*, June

Goodwin, R. M. (1967), in *Socialism, Capitalism and Economic Growth*, A. H. Feinstein (Ed.) (London: Cambridge University Press)

Greater London Council (1974), *Supplementary Licencing* (London: Greater London Council)

Green, H. A. J. (1971), *Consumer Theory* (Harmondsworth: Penguin)

Grey, A. (1975), *Urban Fares Policy* (Farnborough: Saxon House)

Griliches, Z. (1957), Hybrid corn: an exploration in the economics of technological change, *Econometrica*, October

Gwilliam, K. M. and Mackie, P. (1975), *Economics and Transport Policy* (London: Allen and Unwin)

Gwilliam, K. M. *et al.* (1980), *A Comparative Study of European Rail Performance* (London: British Railways Board)

Harberger, A. C. (1954), Monopoly and resource allocation, *Am. Economic Rev. Proc.*, May

Heggie, I. (1972), *Transport Engineering Economics* (Maidenhead: McGraw-Hill)

Henderson, J. M. and Quandt, R. E. (1971), *Microeconomic Theory*, 2nd edn (Maidenhead: McGraw-Hill)

Hensher, D. A. and Stopher, P. R. (1979), *Behavioural Travel Modelling* (London: Croom Helm)

Hicks, J. R. (1956), *A Revision of Demand Theory* (Oxford: Clarendon Press)

Hotelling, H. (1938), The general welfare in relation to problems of taxation and to railway and utility rates, *Econometrica*, July

Intrilligator, M. D. (1971), *Mathematical Optimisation and Economic Theory* (Englewood Cliffs: Prentice-Hall)

Jones, I. D. (1977), *Urban Transport Appraisal* (London: Macmillan)

Joy, S. (1973), *The Train that Ran Away* (London: Ian Allen)

Layard, R. P. G. (1972), *Cost Benefit Analysis* (Harmondsworth: Penguin)

Layard, R. P. G. (1977), The distributional effects of congestion taxes, *Economica*, August

Layard, R. P. G. and Walters, A. A. (1978), *Microeconomic Theory* (New York: McGraw-Hill)

Leibenstein, H. (1966), Allocative efficiency vs. 'X-efficiency', *Am. Economic Rev.*

Lewis, D. L. (1977), Public transport and traffic levels, *J. Transport Economics and Policy*, May

Lichfield, N. (1970), Evaluation methodology of urban and regional plans: a review, *Regional Studies*

Lipsey, R. G. and Lancaster, K. (1956), The general theory of the second best, *Rev. Economic Studies*

London Transport (1975), *London Transport's Corporate Aim Explained* (London: London Transport Executive)

Lotka, A. J. (1925), *Elements of Physical Biology* (Baltimore: Williams and Wilkins)

Malinvaud, E. (1972), *Lectures on Microeconomic Theory* (Amsterdam: North-Holland)

Mansfield, E. (1968), *The Economics of Technological Change* (New York: Norton)

Marshall, A. (1920), *Principles of Economics,* 8th edn (London: Macmillan)

Martin and Voorhees Associates (1980), *Car Ownership Research Project Final Report* (London: Martin and Voorhees Associates)

McFadden, D. (1976), Quantal choice analysis: a survey, *Ann. Economic and Social Measurement*

McKean, R. N. (1968), The use of shadow prices, in *Problems of Public Expenditure Analysis* (Washington: Brookings Institution)

Moggridge, M. (1981), *The Car Market* (London: Pion)

Mohring, H. (1972), Optimisation and scale economics in urban bus transportation, *Am. Economic Rev.,* September

Mohring, H. (1976), *Transportation Economics* (Cambridge, Mass.: Ballinger)

Monopolies Commission (1974), *Cross-Channel Car Ferry Services* (London: HMSO)

Moore, T. G. (1975), Deregulating surface freight transportation, in *Promoting Competition in Regulated Markets,* A. Phillips (Ed.) (Washington: Brookings Institution)

Mulley, C. (1981), Who did they think they were? Mimeograph

Nash, C. A. (1978), Management objectives, fares and service levels in urban bus transportation, *J. Transport Economics and Policy,* January

Nationalised Industries (1967), *White Paper,* Cmnd 3437 (London: HMSO)

Nationalised Industries (1978), *White Paper,* Cmnd 7131 (London: HMSO)

Nickell, S. J. (1979), *The Investment Decisions of Firms* (Cambridge: Cambridge University Press)

Phillips, A. (1975), *Promoting Competition in Regulated Markets* (Washington: Brookings Institution)

Posner, R. A. (1974), Theories of economic regulation, *Bell J. Economics,* Autumn

Price Commission (1978a), *British Railways Board – Increases in Passenger Fares,* HC225 (London: HMSO)

Price Commission (1978b), *London Transport Executive – Increases in Passenger Fares,* HC594 (London: HMSO)

Pryke, R. (1971), *Public Enterprise in Practice* (London: MacGibbon and Kee)

Pryke, R. (1977), The case against subsidies, in *A Policy for Transport?* (London: Nuffield Foundation)

Pryke, R. and Dodgeson, J. (1975), *The Rail Problem an Alternative Strategy* (London: Martin Robertson)

Quandt, R. E. (1970), *The Demand for Travel* (Heath: Lexington)

Quarmby, D. A. (1967), Choice of travel mode for journey to work: some findings, *J. Transport Economics and Policy*

Quarmby, D. A. (1977), *The Contribution of Economic Research to Transport Policy Decisions,* ECMT, September

Rees, R. (1976), *Public Enterprise Economics* (London: Weidenfeld and Nicolson)

Ruggles, N. (1949), Recent developments in the theory of marginal cost pricing, *Rev. Economic Studies*

Samuelson, P. A. (1942), Constancy of the marginal utility of income, in *Studies in Matthematical Economics and Econometrics in Memory of Henry Schultz,* O. Lange *et al.* (Eds) (Chicago: University of Chicago Press)

Seade, J. (1978), Consumer surplus and linearity of Engel curves, *Economic J.,* September

Sherman, R. (1971), Congestion interdependence and urban transit fares, *Econometrica,* May

Smith, R. P. (1974), A note on car replacement, *Rev. Economic Studies*

Smith, R. P. (1975), *Consumer Demand for Cars in the U.S.A.* (Cambridge: Cambridge University Press)

Smith, V. L. (1972), On models of commercial fishing, *J. Political Economy,* June

Stopher, P. R. and Meyburg, A. H. (1975), *Urban Transportation Modeling and Planning* (Lexington: Heath)

Stubbs, P. C., Tyson, W. J. and Dalvi, M. Q. (1980), *Transport Economics* (London: George Allen and Unwin)

Tanner, J. C. (1978), Long-term forecasting of vehicle ownership and road traffic, *J. R. Statist. Soc. Ser.* A

Tanner, J. C. (1979), Choice of model structure for car ownership forecasting, *Crowthorne, Transport and Road Research Laboratory Report* SR523

Thomson, J. M. (1974), *Modern Transport Economics* (Harmondsworth: Penguin)

Transport Policy (1977), *White Paper,* Cmnd 6836 (London: HMSO)

Wallis, K. F. (1972), *Introductory Econometrics* (London: Gray-Mills)

Walters, A. A. (1961), The theory and measurement of private and social cost of highway congestion, *Econometrica*

Walters, A. A. (1979), Costs and scale of bus services, *World Bank Staff Working Paper No. 325,* April

Watson, P. L. and Holland, E. (1977), *Road Pricing in Singapore; Impacts of the Area Licence Scheme,* World Bank, March

Westin, R. B. (1975), Empirical implications of infrequent purchase behaviour in a stock-adjustment model, *Am. Economic Rev.*

Williams, H. C. W. L. (1979), *Travel Demand Forecasting — an Overview of Theoretical Developments,* mimeogr., University of Leeds

Williamson, O. E. (1966), Peak load pricing and optimal capacity under indivisible constraints, *Am. Economic Rev.,* September

Wooton, H. G. and Pick, G. W. (1967), Trips generated by households, *J. Transport Economics and Policy,* May

Index

Abelson, P. W. 76, 104
Advertising 2
Advisory Committee on Trunk
   Road Assessment 60, 108, 109,
   114, 199
Airports 74, 75, 104, 174, 175
Aneuryn-Evans, G. B. 75
Arrival rate 95
Arrow 170

Bailey, N. T. J. 99, 111
Barker, T. C. 183
Barrier to entry 167
Bates, J. 109, 116, 117
Baumol, W. J. 76
Beesley, M. E. 44, 64, 131, 181
Behavioural demand models 127
Bergson, A. 177
Bly, P. H. 4
Borins, S. F. 74
Bradford, P. F. 76
British Road Federation 108
Bruzelius, N. 31, 132

Capacity 63, 66, 68, 69, 87, 103,
   104, 141, 181
Car ownership 109
Cartel 167
Channel Tunnel 65, 71
Chisholm, M. 43, 165, 170
Collings, J. J. 151

Comparative statics 48
Compensated demand function
   22, 24, 82
Compensating variation 27, 28, 31,
   59, 64, 82, 159
Competition 1, 7, 43, 53, 57, 78,
   140, 164, 168, 170
Concavity 18
Congestion 58, 81, 83, 86, 173,
   179, 181
Consumer 1, 13
Consumer surplus 8, 14, 23, 25,
   62, 66, 82, 85, 155
Corporate objectives 147
Cost 6, 159
Cost function 37
Cost benefit analysis 8, 9, 58, 70,
   99
Cost elasticity 61, 161
Cox, D. R. 94
Crew, M. A. 71
Cross-subsidy 150, 172, 181
Currie, J. M. 25

Deaton, A. 14, 27, 109, 123, 126
Debreu, G. 54
Decentralization 146, 158
Demand 1, 8, 13, 17, 20, 22, 29,
   34, 62, 65, 71, 76, 86, 108,
   136, 141, 147

Department of Transport 99, 119,
  120
Depreciation 66, 111, 121, 123,
  144
Discounting 114, 122, 140
Discrete choice 127, 136
Distortion 85
Distribution of incomes 53, 59,
  164
Dodgeson, J. 48
Domencich, T. A. 110, 118, 128,
  131, 135
Dorfman, R. 43, 70, 170
Dupuit, J. 25, 67
Durables 121

Eades, G. C. 181
Economic appraisal 99, 109, 114,
  136, 140
Efficiency 37, 48, 53, 64, 79, 85,
  90, 141, 144, 164, 178
Elasticity 3, 4, 6, 8, 21, 35, 36, 46,
  73, 78, 113, 114, 115, 149,
  151, 177
Equilibrium 48
Euler's theorem 19
Evaluation 1, 8, 9, 10
Expenditure function 24, 83
Externality 58, 62, 173

Fairhurst, M. H. 80
Fares 1
Feldstein, M. S. 155
Fitzgerald, E. V. K. 75
Fixed cost 38, 41, 145, 156
Flowerdew, A. D. J. 76, 104
Foldes, L P. 165, 174
Foster, C. D. 37, 41, 48
Freight, 50, 108, 182
Friedman, M. 29

Gale, D. 43
Georgano, G. N. 182
Giles, G. E. 108, 109, 121

Glaister, S. 11, 18, 36, 42, 49, 65,
  71, 81, 86, 151, 177, 178, 181
Greater London Council 64
Green, H. A. J. 29
Grey, A. 90, 158
Gunn, H. 109, 116, 117
Gwilliam, K. M. 48

Harberger, A. C. 147, 177
Heggie, I. 170
Henderson, J. M. 18
Hensher, D. A. 110
Hicks, J. R. 28
Hicks-Kaldor criterion 59, 64
Holland, E. 65
Homogeneity of Demand 5
Hotelling, H. 28
Household 116

Income distribution 9, 64, 154,
  174
Income effect 22
Income elasticity 1, 4, 113, 115
Indirect utility function 23
Indivisibilities 70, 125, 127, 144,
  171
Inflation 4
Intrilligator, M. D. 42
Investment criteria 1, 140

Jones, I. D. 110
Joy, S. 42, 146

Kleindorfer, P. R. 71, 165, 170

Lagrangian Multiplier *see* Shadow
  price
Lancaster, K. 84
Layard, R. P. G. 10, 43, 54, 57, 64
Leibenstein, H. 177
Lewis, D. L. 80, 81, 86, 178
Licensing 1, 45, 164
Lichfield, N. 60
Lind, R. C. 170

Linear programming 42
Lipsey, R. G. 84
Logistic function 110, 115, 116, 119, 130, 131
Lotka, A. J. 111

McFadden, D. 110, 118, 127, 128, 131, 135
McKean, R. N. 58
Malinvaud, E. 14, 54, 85
Mansfield, E. 112
Marginal cost 6, 34
Marginal cost pricing 10, 11, 43, 54, 57, 61, 67, 78, 84, 87, 143, 156, 157, 160, 172
Marginal product 38, 142
Marginal rate of substitution 39
Marginal revenue 5, 34
Marginal utility of income 23, 26
Marshall, A. 25
Martin and Voorhees Associates 119
Modal choice 127, 130, 131, 132
Moggridge, M. 121, 123
Mohring, H. 102
Money illusion 19
Monopolies Commission 68
Monopoly 7, 8, 10, 39, 44, 57, 74, 140, 165
Moore, T. G. 182
Muellbauer, J. 14, 27, 109, 123, 126
Mulley, C. 183
Murphy, J. A. 25

Nash, C. A. 147, 152
Nationalised Industry White Paper 146
Net present value 140
Nickell, S. J. 144

Operating costs 62, 65, 73, 77, 82, 87, 147
O'Sullivan, P. 43

Pareto optimum 53
Passenger miles 87, 90, 140, 147, 158, 172
Peak 7, 47, 65, 86, 98, 132, 136, 147, 172, 179, 181
Phillips, A. 165
Poisson process 94, 97, 99, 100
Pollution 58
Ports 70
Posner, R. A. 165, 175
Preferences 1, 15
Price Commission 5, 78
Price discrimination 6, 47, 74, 78, 150, 165, 168
Price distortion 152, 158
Private cost 59
Producer 34
Production function 38, 141
Profit 6, 8, 9, 39, 66, 71, 72, 74, 76, 140, 144, 147, 150
Programming 42
Pryke, R. 48, 91, 146
Public enterprise 8, 34, 85, 140

Quandt, R. E. 18, 110
Quarmby, D. A. 87, 131, 147, 154
Queue length 99, 101, 103
Queues 94

Rees, R. 65, 70, 71, 145, 165, 170, 174
Regulation 1, 7, 45, 164
Returns to scale 39, 44, 57, 58, 70, 102, 145, 166
Revenue 5, 34
Road haulage 44
Road pricing 61, 64, 67, 69, 81, 85
Robbins, M. 183
Roberts, M. 109, 116, 117
Roy's identity 23, 26
Ruggles, N. 70

Safety 168
Samuelson, P. A. 29, 43, 70

Saturation 111, 112
Schmitz, A. 25
Seade, J. 25
Second best 80, 86
Service quality 1, 2, 30, 98, 158, 179
Shadow price 18, 58, 67, 73, 80, 142, 148, 149, 156
Sherman, R. 85
Slack variable 66, 77
Slutsky equation 21, 25
Smith, R. P. 124
Smith, V. L. 112
Smith, W. L. 94
Social cost 59
Social welfare function 80
Solow, R. 43, 70
Speed-flow relationship 62, 87
Stochastic process 94
Stock-flow relationship 122
Stopher, P. R. 110
Subsidy 1, 8, 12, 41, 71, 76, 81, 86, 87, 90, 145, 148, 159, 164, 173
Substitution 22, 55, 58
Supply 2, 45

Tanner, J. C. 109, 112, 113, 115, 120, 126
Tax 1, 50, 53, 62, 76, 155, 159, 164

Taxi 44, 74, 101, 102, 103, 104, 167, 169, 181
Toll 11, 59, 67, 69, 73, 167
Traffic commissioners 68, 166, 167, 170, 182
Traffic intensity 99

Uncertainty 71, 114, 141, 169
Unemployment 58
Unions 5
User cost 123
Utility 13, 15, 129, 130, 133, 154

Value of time 31, 87, 101, 103, 131, 136, 159

Waiting time 99, 101, 103
Wallis, K. F. 124
Walters, A. A. 43, 44, 54, 57, 62
Watson, P. L. 65
Weibull distribution 129
Welfare economics 53
Welfare loss 152, 158, 172, 177
Westin 124
Williamson, D. E. 65
Willingness to pay 8, 26, 62, 77, 83, 141
Worsley, T. E. 108, 109, 121